D1501238

thirst

a memoir

Lisa Fierer

www.lisafierer.com

First Printing, 2020

ISBN: 978-0-578-78983-5

Cover and Chapter Design by MarkGelotte.com

Printed in the United States of America

For my mom,
Mary Ellen Ruth Bailey Fierer

And for anyone who has lived
in fear inside their own home.

It is also for those of us who
have struggled with forgiveness
as we find our way in the world.

"We forgive mostly not from strength but through imperfections, for memory wears transparent as glass with the pattern washed off, till we stare past what injured us.

We forgive because we too have done the same to others easy as a mudslide; or because anger is a fire that must be fed and we are too tired to rise and haul a log."

— Marge Piercy

AUTHOR'S NOTE

This book is dedicated to the stories within each of us and the hope that we may be heard and acknowledged. I believe that when we shine light into the dark crevices within ourselves that we touch a place that connects us all. The details of our particular devastation may differ but the pain is the same. And in that vulnerability we each have a choice: to move towards the light or shrink in the shadows.

Memoir is only true to the lived experience of one individual, the author. All of the events in this memoir are real, but this story holds only my memories of those events from my own perspective, supported by public articles and legal documents. Everyone else who appears in this story has their own memories, their own perspective and their own truth. One story and one truth does not negate or diminish anyone else's. I have chosen to change the names of certain individuals, groups and locations in order to protect their privacy. Expressing my own truth and my own experience is both terrifying and incredibly healing. I hope this book will encourage you to share your own.

CHAPTER 1

Fragments of bone and flakes of ash filled my hands. The humidity of India in August was fusing the viscous powder to my skin. I wanted to fling it off my fingers, shake the sludge from my hands and at the same time, clutch onto it forever. These ashes and fragments were all that was left of my father. Even though I'd spent most of my thirty four years of life hating him, letting go of him felt like the hardest thing I would ever do.

As I stood on the edge of the Ganges river, about to release my father to the water, I remembered my Sanskrit teacher Kari told me, "The Ganga is sacred. When you release the ashes of the deceased into the River, it frees the karmic load of your ancestors for seven generations past and seven generations into the future." If anyone needed freedom from his karmic load, it was my father.

Two days earlier, while in the Denver International Airport, I used all of the strength in my 5' 4" body to heave my carry-on bag—carrying my father—onto the security conveyor belt. Dad's remains weighed at least twenty pounds and took up most of the space in my bag. Inside the bag, Dad looked like a nicely wrapped Christmas gift. A16"x16" flat, square envelope constructed of sturdy handmade paper with dried roses and wildflowers pressed into its flesh. The funeral home told me the paper was "designed to disintegrate in a timely and ecological manner." The funeral home told me that my Dad's ashes would be FedEx'd to me prior to my departure for India.

The funeral home told me the word for the ashes and flakes that my father had become: Cremains. I liked how that word felt on my tongue. Cremains. Saying it made me feel grown up, somehow, cremains.

As I took off my shoes and placed them on the conveyor belt, awaiting my turn to walk through the full-body scanner, I handed my dad's death certificate to the security guard who stood about six feet tall, with a neatly trimmed afro, her entire body blocking the full-body scanner.

Then, I gestured to my bag that had already started to make its way into the luggage scanner and casually dropped my new favorite word, "My father's cremains are in that bag," I told her, "I'm taking them to India."

Her eyes simultaneously softened and tensed up as she intercepted my bag—my dad—and announced, "Honey, I'm gonna need you to step over here," gesturing to a small holding area to the side of the security line.

"Ok, honey..." she sighed, "Here's what you need to know: when ashes pass through the scanner they register as explosives," She could tell I wasn't registering what she was saying, so she added, "Bomb material."

Hearing the word "bomb" said by a TSA agent made me giddy and nervous. It was as if my chubby, white-haired third grade teacher, Mrs. Huxford, had included the word "fuck" in a spelling bee.

"Bomb?!" I said, almost shouting.

"Yes," she whispered, encouraging me to whisper, too. "Sit tight," she added and quickly left my side.

I could see her opening my bag and waving a wand over my father, like a sorceress summoning... something. *An apology? A better dad? A do-over?*

"You're fine, Honey," she announced, "Have a good trip."

I put on my shoes, shouldered the weight of my carry-on, and headed down the escalator to the train. But those two words got stuck in my brain: *Bomb. Explosive.* Ringing loudly in my mind, throughout my body. *Bomb. Explosive.* My whole body began to shake. *Bomb. Explosive.* That was my dad, alright.

Sometimes my father would walk through the front door of our family home whistling. I thought this was an indication of joy, of my father being happy, of our home being safe. But by the age of three, I realized that my father's whistling was a prelude to an explosion. The only spark needed was for my father to see something out of place. A chair untucked from the dining room table. A candlestick off center. The radio too loud. My mother happy. That's when he would explode. Throwing chairs, candlesticks, radios at walls and windows, at bodies. Throwing my brother's body against the walls and windows. Throwing my mother up against the wall. All it took was something off-center to detonate my father.

"Dinesh, sir, I have my father's ashes with me and I wish to release them at some point during my travels if that's ok?" my voice cracked as I asked my guide, shortly after meeting him at the New Delhi airport. Dinesh nodded with reverence and certainty, "Yes, of course. We'll arrange for it in two days' time, at the most perfect place."

What was I doing? I didn't know Dinesh from Brahma! I'd never been to the Ganges, as far as I knew, he could have taken me to a local fishing hole instead of a sacred river to dump my dad. The only thing I knew was that I needed a guide and he was mine, so I asked.

Two days later Dinesh announced the 'perfect place.' The location is called Har ki Pauri in Hindi, which translates, "to place one's ancestors at God's feet." Har ki Pauri is the exit point of the river Ganges from the mountains as it enters into the plains.

Dinesh negotiated the cost of the ritual with a priest in rapid fire Hindi, and now standing on the banks of the river, I wondered if the wildflowers in the biodegradable paper really would dissolve.

The Brahmin Priest's "office", a small 10x10 plywood shack that had been painted bright blue, was one of many lining the banks of the River. I gazed across the river, which spanned the width of a football field and my eyes settled on a Brahmin Priest in the midst of a ceremony. His wrists swirled in pools of clockwise movement. Like the conductor of an orchestra of spirits, he was fueled by faith.

I felt lightheaded and took a deep breath, inhaling the faint smell of turmeric. The warm brown water of the Ganges River looked thick as it held up floating marigolds and vibrant red poppies. There were circles of purple and orange and red staying afloat, blurring together as my eyes filled with tears. Lining the banks of the river were women wearing teal, pink, red saris and men wearing white kurtas; Hindu people of all ages, entire families, standing on the banks of both sides of the river with Brahmin Priests conducting the same ceremony. All of them were letting go of someone, too.

To my surprise, my Brahmin Priest looked like most of the guys my father grew up with in Brooklyn. *Aw,* I thought, *what an awesome thing, my dad would appreciate the connection.* The Brahmin was wearing a crisp white button-down shirt and navy pleated dress pants. He had steel blue eyes and wore a circular covering on the top of his head, which looked like the yarmulkes my grandpa and great-uncles wore on the Sabbath.

For the next thirty minutes, this Brooklyn Brahmin chanted in Sanskrit, recitations for releasing a relative. It was easy to relax into the hypnotic rhythm of his chanting, catching a word or two that I understood from my Sanskrit studies.

He handed the package that contained my father's cremains to his assistant, a tall skinny teenage boy wearing a dhoti. With his bare hands, the boy ripped open the package, grabbing a canvas bag inside and handing me the wrapping paper to deal with. *Holy shit!* I thought, I *paid a small fortune for that packaging.* I didn't know what to do with it and it didn't seem like a good time to ask, so I shoved it into my backpack. The boy held up the canvas bag and in one quick, SWOOSH, sliced its soft belly open with a razor blade. I could see the blade glint in the sunlight; the irony of someone slicing into what remained of my father was not lost on me. Twenty-four years earlier, my father's hands held a blade aimed at my mother.

The priest motioned for me to hold out my hands. The priest-in-training upended the contents into my cupped hands. The ashes were mottled grey, with pure white pieces of bone scattered throughout. Fragments of ash clung to my long shirt-dress, the kind that Indian women often wear over pants. Mine was red and gold, with tiny mirrors sewn into the fabric, each mirror reflecting this mystifying ritual.

The priest interrupted his chanting and spoke very emphatically in Hindi to Dinesh. With a sideways bob of his head, the Indian equivalent of nodding, Yes, my guide turned to me and translated, "He says pray from your Heart."

How does this Brahmin priest, who doesn't even speak the same language as me, know I'm stuck in my head? Until I heard him say that, I had never considered the origin of my prayers. I pressed a large piece of ash, the shape of a frosted flake, between my index finger and thumb and began to sob. Taking a deep breath, filling my belly and chest, for the first time I felt my prayers emanating from my heart. I began to understand then what my life would continue to teach me: prayer transcends all language.

The priest motioned me forward as I slowly opened my hands and released the ashes into the murky brown water of the Ganges, inviting it to swallow Dad up, to drink him in.

As the current began to carry my father downriver washing away his karmic burden, I realized that the act of letting go was also washing away something I didn't know was possible.

Dad, I forgive you for killing Mom. I release you. I release me.

CHAPTER 2

I learned how to read my father's eyes in the rearview mirror. There weren't many things we did as a family, but we did take road trips from Morton, Illinois to Aspen, Colorado where Dad attended an annual Pathology Conference. It was the summer of 1979 when we piled into the white, wood-paneled Pontiac station wagon to head out west. At seven years old, my mind filled with wonder at the ability of the Rocky Mountains to keep their tips covered in snow, even when it was 85 degrees and sunny.

Mom rode shotgun, with my older brother Jonny and me fitting comfortably in the carpeted space between the back seat and bumper; the trunk, I guess, but at the time it felt like a lush playground. We pressed our mouths into huge O shapes against the foggy back window; making faces at the other drivers, staring them down in an attempt to make them change lanes. The only power we possessed at seven and ten was that of annoyance, so we wielded it as much as possible.

Our older sisters, Robin and Sue sat in the back seat, Robin twirling her dirty-blonde hair incessantly and Sue—the oldest of us all—doing her best to ignore us by listening to music. Her new transistor radio with headphones ate up half of her head.

As always, Mom sat in the passenger seat doing macramé while Dad drove, watching Jonny and me in the rearview mirror. I kept trying to look at Dad's eyes without him catching me. When they got that cold, faraway look, I knew to be afraid. But if he had the faraway look and his pupils were dilated it was okay; he was just daydreaming. The difference between fear and dreaming was in the size of his pupils.

Right now, I am having difficulties remembering what happens next. Is that ok? Will you still stay in the car with me? My family? I've learned that trauma survivors have fragmented and incomplete memories. So, sometimes, I remember things in small broken parts, in snapshots. I remember my father moving the mirror to look at us, but not to see us, more like he was tracking us. Monitoring our moves so that they didn't infringe upon his mood. The one thing I do remember in this moment, is how our last name is pronounced. Fierer is pronounced, Fear. And that we lived in Morton, Illinois in a house that looked like a peach.

Our house was a peach-colored two-story brick ranch with an unfinished basement that housed my father's coveted wine cellar. Dad was a Doctor, Dr. Joshua Allen Fierer. A professor of Pathology at the medical school at the University of Illinois, where he also ran a cancer research lab. My mom, Mary Ellen Ruth Bailey Fierer, had beautiful red hair, freckles, green eyes, and was an opera singer. She wrote for the small local paper, The Courier. It was by far the most banal thing about her otherwise eccentric nature.

In my grade school years, Mom's less-than-typical behavior lent itself to my constant embarrassment: her Soprano singing of the National Anthem at our local football games, writing messages for teachers in circles so they would have to spin it around to decipher, and her wearing of costumes for no particular reason or occasion. Some of Mom's favorite costumes included: The Beef-eater and a Pepto-Bismol pink bunny rabbit. That's right, when all of my friend's mothers were wearing muumuu's or sweat suits, my mother donned an exaggerated black top hat, opaque red tights, thick red knee-length jacket with dark blue and gold trimmings, and complete with a ceremonial (fake) spear, drove me to school.

There's a photo of our family that really captures the odd spirit of the Fierers. It was taken by our neighbors and my parents' close friends, Marty and Cindy Channing. Cindy arranged us all in front of our fireplace as if we were dolls in a dollhouse. Dad, the Republican, in the right corner, looms about six inches over my liberal mom. Both dressed in black as if on their way to a funeral, they weren't touching each other at all. Dad was staring, deadpan at the camera, his pupils constricted, his lips slightly parted, barely revealing his front teeth. Mom's red hair softly curled to frame her face, her left eyebrow raised, as if she was just about to say something. Sue stood between them looking out from beneath her long brown bangs. Her attempt at a smile turned into an expression of concern. Robin stood directly in front of Dad, his hands resting lovingly on her shoulders. Far to the left was Jonny, lanky with a mop of sun-streaked hair that moved like fire; his head completely turned to the left, like he could see something just out of the frame and wanted to run towards it. As the youngest, I was directly in the center. My pudgy, four-year-old arms hung thick by my sides, my blue eyes open wide as I grinned at the camera. As confident as I looked in that particular photo, it was fleeting.

Everything outside of the frame of the photo felt scary. Everyone in that photo was afraid of something. Except for Dad. He wasn't afraid of anything. I remember Robin and me sharing a bedroom around this time. Our bunk beds were hot pink. I slept on the bottom and Robin on the top. There was a slight gap between the beds and the wall. I was afraid of this space, of what could be lurking inside of it.

Mom made two long bolsters covered in matching hot pink furry material to protect me from the scary gap between the edge of my mattress and the wall. Most nights at bedtime, I would step on the bolsters and stick my head up to visit with Robin. One school night when I was in second grade and Robin was in seventh grade, I was standing on the firm bolsters, resting my chin on the edge of Robin's mattress, telling her how much I hated Physical Education class. "We had the President's Test today and I didn't pass. Why do we have to do those stupid things like pull ups and running?" All of a sudden, our bedroom door opened. The second I saw the top of mom's head, the fluff of her hair, the color of a nearly ripe orange, I shut my eyes and slumped my head on Robin's mattress. As if I was fast asleep. Standing up. I heard Mom pause. "Lis, honey, I know you're asleep," she swallowed a giggle, "but I think you'll be more comfortable laying down, okay?"

Robin was completely terrified of eyeballs. Every night she would place small pieces of pre-cut paper over all the eyes on all the posters in our room including the innocuous Muppets. "I don't like them looking at me!" she said emphatically. Robin had Orphan Annie sheets and used a black marker to color in all of Orphan Annie's eyeballs.

In spite of the oddly eyeballed Orphan Annie sheets, I always longed to sleep on the top bunk. Before leaving for summer camp at Interlochen, a music camp in Michigan, Robin made me coupons. They were written in brightly colored puffy paint on rectangles she had cut out of construction paper. Little construction paper envelopes were included with the coupons so that I could mail them to her Prior To Using, per her rules. The coupons read: "Valid for one night sleeping in Robbie's bed (must change sheets after use)" and "Can take 1 nap in Robbie's bed (must change sheets after use)". Robin knew that I desperately wanted the top bunk, and even though she was scared of heights, as the older sister, she got dibs. Robin wasn't spiteful, but as a middle child, who could blame her for enjoying the power opportunities of sibling birth order. I innately respected my lower rank in this unspoken hierarchy and, out of fear of retaliation, I followed her rules to a 'T'.

We always joked that Sue was the milkman's daughter because she was the only one of us who had brown eyes and straight brown hair, while the other three of us siblings are blue-eyed, curly haired blondes. When she got her learner's permit, Sue would charge us a quarter if we wanted to go with her to get ice cream, or if we needed a ride somewhere and our mom couldn't take us. She was a cheerleader and one of the most popular girls at Morton High School. Her fears remain a mystery to me, but she must have had them because she's part of our family.

Although my brother Jonny and I are closest in age, we were physically polar opposites. At ten years old, he looked like a very tall toothpick with thick, floppy hair that threatened to tip him over. This was in spite of the fact that he ate nonstop. Multiple breakfasts, lunches and dinners, he couldn't shovel it in fast enough. Jonny loved to be the center of attention, an artist with a free spirit who shined most when he was painting or dancing around the house. My Dad referred to Jonny's uninhibited nature as, "annoying." The only thing Jonny was afraid of was our father. When he was eight or nine, Jonny custom painted each of the folding chairs in our basement; they were beautiful. Everyone thought so, except for Dad who grabbed him by the neck and lifted him up in the air, throwing him down and beating the shit out of him for the infraction of being creative. This was only one reason why Jonny feared Dad.

Back in the car, in 1979, we're still on our way to Aspen;

Jonny and I have managed to convince a third car to change lanes because of the wonderfully obnoxious faces we are making from the window in the trunk. Bonus: the driver, a twenty something guy wearing a Wisconsin Badgers red knit hat with a giant white pom pom rolled his eyes as he zipped into the other lane. Jonny and I laughed so hard I nearly peed. Just then, Dad said in a loud voice, "Lisa, come up here!" My heart dropped. My body hesitated for a second, but I knew I'd only get in more trouble if I didn't move, so I hoisted my leg over the backseat, accidentally kicking Robin's shoulder. She swiped at me like a feral cat, glaring at me as I fell onto Sue's lap. Sue took a different tack, offering me a smirk and pushing my bum to usher me up front.

Sitting between my parents, I marveled at the fact that they were both singing to the same song on the radio, but the only indication that it was the same song was the words; there was no harmony. Dad's falsetto voice, falling out of his large mouth, his large face, everything about him seemed larger than the rest of us. His hazel eyes rolled back along with his head as he shrilled at the top of his lungs, nearly drowning out Mom's well-trained Soprano voice.

Did he think he had a good voice? Or did he just have to over-power mom in any way possible? Maybe both.

I tried looking out the window, to avoid the discomfort of being stuck between shrill and soprano. My gaze stopped short of the window and rested on my Dad's hand which was perched on the steering wheel. His hands were average in size: not particularly strong, yet not weak. His thumbs were stubby, like mine, only he didn't have to deal with the ruthless teasing by my siblings, "you were born without thumbs so they sewed big toes on to your hands." Out of shame, I'd hide them, folding them into the center of my palms and wrapping my four fingers around. I wished I'd inherited my mom's hands. Her fingers were long and graceful, with perfectly shaped fingernails. I loved her hands. The veins on her right met in confluence to create the letter "K". In a loving but sassy way, I'd often respond to her motherly requests (to pick up my room, do my homework, practice violin, etc.) by making the shape of "O" with one of my hands and placing it beside her right hand. Saying "O-kay Mom."

Another snapshot. It's the week before Christmas 1979 and my dad is away on a business trip.

Mom had a twinkle in her green eyes when she picked Jonny and me up from school that wintery Thursday evening. "I have a great idea..." she paused, the excitement building in her voice, "since Dad's away, we'll get a Christmas tree this year. We can decorate it, and put it on the landing. We'll just be sure and take it down before he comes home." We cheered and began discussing the details of dressing the tree.

For the first six years of my life we'd celebrate both Christmas and Hanukkah. My father was Jewish, my mom had been raised Protestant and, perhaps as a stipulation to marry my father, converted to Judaism. But then, when her mother passed away, Christmas disappeared without explanation. Although Mom was the only freckled Irish person in the temple, she mastered learning Hebrew, all the traditions, and the Torah.

Morton was a Christian town, a place of clean streets, manicured lawns and church-going Christians. I would crack myself up by inventing billboards for Morton like, "The Quality of Your Lawn is More Important Than The Reality of Your Life," or, "Better to Save Your Face than Your Ass".

I had my own relationship with religion, with what I called

God. Just a name that rhymes with odd to explain all those unex-
plainable things and uncanny occurrences. I prayed every night
and talked to God, in my head. My constant prayer was, *God,*
please make my dad stop hitting my mom and my brother so we can all
feel safe in our home.

Standing in our manicured front yard in Morton, Illinois,
shivering and rubbing our arms with our hands as snowflakes
made tufts on our heads. All of us, except for Dad, looked at our
glorious—and forbidden—Christmas tree that we placed on the
five foot landing pad halfway up the stairs to the second story.
We had covered it in as many ornaments as we could find, but it
still looked more like a Charlie Brown Christmas tree.

I never heard my dad's car in the driveway that night, and it
wasn't until the wee hours of the morning that I suspected Dad
had returned from his trip early. Due to the countless times Dad
yelled at midnight, banging down bedroom doors, usually Jonny's,
I had become a light sleeper and woke up instantly when I heard
the faint noise of a crack. To someone outside our home it might
have sounded like a wooden vase falling off a shelf, only I knew
that sound. It was my Dad's thick fist hitting my mom.

The crack was coming from my parent's bedroom. *Was it safe*
to get up and check? Should I try to get to the phone and call 911, once
again? Or was it just a bad dream? The little hairs on my arms were
standing up, telling me to pull the covers over my head and wait
it out. At seven years-old I both knew what to do and didn't know
what to expect.

The next day I discovered our Christmas tree was gone. There
was not a needle or an ornament in sight. That morning I tried
to ignore the familiar thick air in the house, like the heaviness
of humidity lingering after a sudden downpour. My father was

whistling, supposedly happy to be home early from a work trip to spend time with his family. My mom wore a big wool sweater even though the heat was turned on high and sunglasses. I knew that underneath those sunglasses was a black eye. I had learned that when Mom wore sunglasses inside the house after hearing a crack in the middle of the night, she had a black eye. I took note and decided to study her eyes, like I did when driving with my father.

Mom must have taken the hit silently, with just the faintest of sounds uncontrollably leaking out of her mouth, as to not wake us. But this time I was really pissed off - way more than a seven year old should ever be. I sat down on the floor of my bedroom with a big pile of red and green construction paper and began to make my own tree. I methodically cut out long strips of paper and taped them together to create floor to ceiling length chains, which I hung from the light fixture in my room. I had to use a chair and all the hardback books I could find piled on top to reach the metal loop that connected the light fixture to the ceiling. The rhythmic cutting and connecting of the links calmed me down, making me feel less helpless. I wanted to prove a point but I didn't want to set my room on fire, so I sat by the paper chain tree nervously, waiting for my dad. Mom peeked in on me, she was moving slowly, which made me think she'd received more than a black eye. "Are you ok?" she asked quietly. "Yeah, Mom, I'm okay," I scanned her as I answered to see if she was really all right, strengthening my resolve to stand up to Dad.

Out of nowhere, Dad appeared like a shadow behind Mom in my bedroom doorway. His black frizzy crew cut loomed a few inches above my mom's red curls. I was grateful I couldn't see his eyes. In contrast to his curious silence I yelled "You can tear down this tree too if you want, but you can't steal Christmas!" I took a deep breath waiting for his reaction. Nothing. He simply turned and left. I felt like I'd won.

My dad's rage was unpredictable, like a pane of glass suddenly shattering. A part of me always knew that it could come crashing down, and the other part wanted to avoid looking up, knowing shards of glass land indiscriminately. I'd learn years later that there is a distinct pattern to the cycle of violence. The buildup was like watching a Tsunami growing a mile from the shore, picking up stamina and suctioning as much water as possible into its wave curl, only to hurl itself and all its contents with as much force as possible onto the helpless sand. Then it would retreat as quickly as it had stormed through, the weight of its force having consumed everything in its path.

I'm sorry, I can't get back into our white Pontiac station wagon. I can't remember how that car ride to Aspen ends, but I can tell you about a time when my father's car stealthily pulled into the driveway of my friend Mandy's house. I can tell you about that because that memory is clear.

One day when I was eight, I was playing at my friend Mandy's house after school. We were outside in her yard, immersed in an adventure game we made up, on a secret mission in the Arctic, searching for 'undiscovered ice territory.' Mandy was a polar bear, waiting behind a glacier (a maple tree) to scare me as I conducted research of the wild terrain (their tennis courts).

I didn't hear my father pull into her driveway. I was used to the sound of his little blue Fiat, but it never occurred to me that he would actually drive the 500 feet from our house around the corner to Mandy's house. Her mom, Mrs. Sloninger, sporting her usual hair bun, perched high on her head like a dinner roll, came out into the yard to get me, saying, with a worried but compassionate look, "Lisa, your father just drove over, he needs you to come home with him." Mrs. Sloninger had waist-length brown hair and when I slept over at Mandy's I loved the rare moments when I got to see her hair cascading all the way to her butt as she took it down for the night. But during the day it was always in the bun, managed and restrained and coiled politely, just like everything else in Morton.

Upon seeing my father, I noticed he wore the same suit that he'd worn to work earlier that morning. It was the color of freshly poured cement. He was completely silent, a very bad sign. Hurrying to his car I felt like I was walking the plank; I had gone from pretending to be afraid while playing Arctic with Mandy, to being consumed by fear of my father. Tunelessly whistling as he silently drove, I watched him carefully out of the corner of my eye. The tension in my stomach felt tight all the way up into my forehead. Even though it was the middle of summer and my legs were sticking to the butterscotch colored leather seats in his Fiat, I felt chilled all over. He parked in our driveway, turned off the engine and made me sit there for a long moment.

"Do you know why I had to come pick you up?" he asked. He wasn't yelling, in fact his voice was cold and formal.

"Nope." I said, trying not to swallow hard.

He didn't say a word and didn't look at me, just made me sit there even longer, waiting. In the thick stillness, I thought about Mr. Capinus, my third-grade science teacher who was talking today about black holes, and how there's such a strong pull in them that even light can't get out. Sitting in my dad's car in our driveway felt like I was stuck in a black hole. Finally, my dad said, "Come with me, I'll show you."

Following my father into the house we walked down the long

hallway to the room I shared with Robin. Our bunk beds were set directly in front of the window. He sat on my bed and patted next to him for me to sit down and look.

"Now do you see? " he asked me.

But I didn't. All I saw was the top of my hot pink bolsters and the bottom part of the window.

Sitting there, I wasn't sure what I was supposed to be looking at. In my confusion and fear, I didn't know what to do with my legs. So, I crossed them, then uncrossed them, then... I couldn't shake the feeling that something wasn't right. At eight years old, I didn't comprehend why it was so strange to be sitting on my bed with my dad. But it was.

Finally, exasperated, he said loudly, "Can you see that you left the window open?"

I looked and sure enough, it was open just a few inches, not even all the way. And to see it he would have had to be sitting on my bed. Exactly where I was now. Why would he come home from work, come into my room, and sit on the edge of the bed? He raised his voice even more. "Do you know the air conditioning is on? Do you know how much it costs to run that air conditioning? Do you know how hard I work to make sure that there's a roof over our heads, food on the table, and luxuries like air conditioning?" The questions spewed out of his mouth in one rapid gush, like the flood from the garden hose when I'd forgotten to turn off the water before detaching the sprinkler. As if to answer his own rhetorical questions, he went on, " I work incredibly hard to provide for a family of six, and make sure that you all have nice things, music lessons, ballet lessons, swim team (*I never was on the swim team, just Jonny,* but kept this thought to myself) and cheerleading (Again, I remained silent, thinking, *only Sue was a cheerleader, and Robin was on Drill Team).*

My thoughts were interrupted by the sudden silence. He was waiting for me to say, I'm sorry, but I wasn't. So, we sat there until he stood up. Just as I'd studied his eyes in the rearview mirror, I noticed the way the muscles beneath his cheeks tightened and loosened like he was gritting his teeth, and how his knuckles turned white as he balled his hands into fists. I felt fairly certain that he wouldn't hit me. For some unspoken reason, he seemed to reserve that violence for Mom and Jonny. I wasn't sorry, just scared and sad. I had opened the window that morning to let a lightning bug out, but it didn't work because the screen was in the way. Dad walked away muttering loudly under his breath, continuing his diatribe about how much he did for all of us and how no one was grateful.

I didn't know it then, but one day, Jonny, my mother and I would pull that screen out and climb through that same window when we left my father for good.

CHAPTER 3

Most kids don't get to take dead body parts to school, but I did. It was a Monday in the middle of fall. I loved the fall in Morton for lots of reasons; one was that our town was the self-proclaimed "pumpkin capital of the world". We had a giant Libby's plant in the center of town, whose sole purpose was to process and can the truckloads of pumpkins that filled up our fields from August until November. The Pumpkin Pageant was held every year at the fairgrounds and this year, as a proud Fourth grader and an official Pumpkin Pageant princess, I boasted a fake rhinestone tiara. My mom had hand sewn my pageant dress: a grey blue silky gown patterned with black musical notes and poofy 80's sleeves, as well as my 'talent' outfit: A Snoopy costume made of felt, complete with a snout that strapped beneath the head. I loved it. Even though it was over ninety degrees in that costume, I was ready to play my violin with all the vigor of Snoopy himself! Years of symphony practice—and love of cartoons—had prepared me for this pageant moment.

The pageant went well, I think, but now my thoughts are taken to a few days afterwards, when pageantry and politeness were no longer on the menu. And my father was picking me up from symphony.

Dad picked me up from symphony rehearsal. I hadn't made any obvious mistakes in practice, and couldn't wait to tell him about it so he would praise me. But he barely acknowledged my chattering as we zipped through town in his bright blue Fiat, so I tried another approach:

"Dad, I have to bring something for Show and Tell on Friday, got any ideas?"

I'd already learned that he was much more engaged if something got to be his idea and this time it worked. In fourth grade I hated multiplication tables, but I loved Show and Tell, which occurred every other Friday in Ms. Henderson's class.

He looked right at me, "sure, Flea bop! Would you like to bring something from the lab?"

I wasn't particularly interested in all the gross stuff that filled the pathology laboratory where he worked at the University in Peoria and I had only a vague interest in the workings of the body. I did like looking at my own earwax under the microscope that Dad had given me; despite my frustration with the precision of setting up the glass slides.

"Yeah Dad!" I said, with as much enthusiasm as I could muster. "What do you think would be good to bring?"

"Well," he said "we're doing some studies right now in the lab on Lung Cancer." He looked at me sternly and pointed at me with his left middle finger. "You know how horribly disgusting smoking is, right ?"

I had a sudden picture of him smoking his pipe every night after dinner and remembered the explanation he gave, "You don't inhale when smoking a pipe, it's not at all like cigarettes." He was the doctor-lung-cancer-research-guy, but it always seemed a bit off to me.

He took both hands off the steering wheel to turn to me and exclaim, "I got it!" I nervously watched to make sure he put at least one hand back on the wheel. "You could bring a real diseased lung to school! The kids will love that!" He was serious and seemed completely thrilled with himself. "Oh, that's a great idea," I said, struggling to keep my voice even.

By Thursday I had forgotten about it, but my dad had an incredible memory for details. That evening, he came home from work and presented me with a gallon sized sealed bag filled with grey fluid. And a lung! Inside the murky water, barely staying afloat was an actual, human, brown and black speckled lung. My gag reflex kicked in as I held back the urge to vomit on the spot. Knowing that if I expressed any opposition to my father's 'brilliant' idea, he would explode, I took the diseased lung from him and said "thanks Dad, I'm sure I'll get an awesome grade!" As I left the kitchen with this this Thing, anxiety started to form a pit in my stomach and I could only hope that that pit didn't end up in another fourth grader's Show and Tell moment.

My mom and three siblings were in the kitchen getting dinner ready. None of them screamed or yelled and absolutely no one told my dad that a diseased lung floating in formaldehyde stuffed in a big zip lock might not be appropriate for Show and Tell. Everyone should have looked and pointed and realized it was insane, but no one did, which is I guess, its own kind of crazy. It was just one more thing that wasn't normal.

We pretended it was.

I stored the lung in the fridge that night, wedged between a gallon of milk and leftover lasagna. I carried it to school the next day in a small red plastic cooler that my dad brought from the lab, and slid it under my desk until Show and Tell started that afternoon.

My classmates brought all kinds of stuff to Show and Tell; a whole house built of Popsicle sticks, a small plastic bathtub frog and other random kid junk. I was fourth in line, but before standing I reached under my desk and opened the cooler. The smell hit me right away, burning the inside of my nose, making my eyes water.

When I lifted the bag out I knew that the bag had broken and the formaldehyde was leaking everywhere. My classmates yelled and held their noses, backing away from my cooler. My teacher came to my desk and looked down at the cooler, gasping for air. She carried it over to the big metal sink in the back corner of the room and held up the bag, looking like she too was about to throw up. Thick syrupy grey fluid was leaking out of the bottom.

"Is this a Lung?" she asked me, horrified.

I nodded, tears filling my eyes, shame burning in my stomach, like this was all my fault. My brother probably would have enjoyed this; he loved shocking people. But I was just the opposite, I just wanted to be normal and fit in. I had hoped that bringing the lung would be cool or very interesting at worst, after all, nobody else's dad worked with dead bodies. This was a big deal for my father, who had come up with a great idea and he would be pleased with me for having helped execute it. But now I was just embarrassed. The teacher didn't say anything else, just lowered the leaking bag into the cooler and cancelled the rest of the Show and Tell for the day. In a way, her reaction made me feel a bit better. She was an adult having a normal reaction to something crazy, not like my parents who always pretended everything was ok. I wanted her to see how insane my dad was. I wanted our family secrets to leak out of the cooler and into my teacher's awareness so she could cancel the rest of my fear, cancel my father punching my mother.

I realize now that I had a strong sense of right and wrong. I knew that taking a diseased lung to school was a bad idea, but it would take me many more decades to learn how to listen to my own intuition and how to say no. Even to my father.

When I got home I knew my dad would be waiting to hear how it went. "How did it go at Show and Tell?" he asked me, "was my lung a smash hit?" I could have lied but I told him the truth. "It leaked," I said, "It leaked everywhere and everyone smelled it and my teacher cancelled the Show and Tell and now everyone thinks I'm a freak."

"Those uneducated ingrates," he said, his hazel eyes squinting dangerously into horizontal lines "they don't even know how to appreciate the honor of higher education!"

"Are you serious Dad?" I asked. I knew I was skating on thin ice, but I had to try to speak up.

His voice became cold and sharp, "And after All I've done for You, you apparently don't appreciate it either!"

I knew it was best to let my dad have the last word, he always found a way to have it anyway. My mom didn't try to referee the fight; she just found a trash bag to put the leaking lung into and placed the cooler in the garage so my dad could take it back to work. "It's fine," she said before I went to bed that night, handing me her favorite book of yoga poses, the one with the skinny Indian guy on the cover. "Next week you can take my yoga book to Show and Tell."

"Thanks Mom," I said, both of us falling into silent recognition that, as always, she had to clean up my father's mess.

Sitting on the end of my bed, about to tuck me in, my mom suddenly got that sparkle in her eye, "Do you want to put your stuffed animals under your sheets and come stay with me in Jonny's room? We can make it like a slumber party!" I can't quite recall a time when my parents actually both slept in the master bedroom. At some point my mom had moved into my brother Jonny's room and was relocated to the basement.

There was an edge to her voice that told me that it wouldn't really be like a slumber party at all. And while I cherished the time

I got to spend alone with Mom, I knew that she wanted me to sleep with her to protect her from my dad. I tried to think of it as a game – a kind of hide and seek. I felt a huge obligation to protect my mom, but it also made me resentful, I was the youngest, after all. Why was it my job to protect her from my raging, violent and unpredictable dad? But I always tried to break up their fights. From the time I was four years old, I had been jumping in the middle as he would beat my mom or brother, pounding my tiny fists against my dad's back to try to get him to stop. I was usually the one who called the police. So, when my mother asked me to stay with her, I simply agreed and tucked my stuffed animals under the sheet in my bed until they looked like my own body. Then I went to sleep with her in Jonny's room, although neither of us slept very much at all.

By the next Sunday, when my dad picked us up from Sunday school at the Synagogue, I could tell that something was wrong. The air in the car was sharper than usual, like it could cut itself with itself. I'm sure Jonny felt it too, because he jumped into the back seat, leaving me stuck in the front, my mind full of questions: *Was our father bored? Angry? Was it a bad day or a good one? And why was He picking us up and not mom?* I stole a sideways glance at him, searching for any clues. His expression was frozen, dazed almost, wearing a sinister smile.

"Your mother has some nice tan lines," he said suddenly – more to the driver's side window than to us. I felt my stomach lurch the way it did when I dreamt I was falling and I couldn't wake up.

"She sure looks good with some sun." his voice trailed off. I knew they hadn't slept in the same bedroom in years. How would he know about her tan lines?

Dad had barely stopped the car in the driveway when I jumped out to go and find Mom, the toe of my sneaker nearly catching on the door rim of his Fiat.

She was in the laundry room, frantically pushing a huge load of clothes into the washer. Her red hair was disheveled, there were sticks and leaves stuck in it; she looked like she had been rolling in the dirt in the field next to our house. Her long slender hands were trembling, the freckles on her fingers in a nervous dance. "Mom! Are you ok? Why didn't you pick us up at Sunday school? What's wrong?" I put my hand gently on her arm, and tried to see her eyes.

"He raped me," she said quietly.

"What?"

This was my first exposure to what most kids get as the 'birds and the bees talk'. I may have sucked at Math, but at eight years old, I was smart enough to piece together what it meant. She saw me deciphering the meaning and said, "Yes, Honey. Your father forced me to have sex with him. I tried to get away; he pinned me down."

She set down the armful of white clothes and turned to face me, "I finally escaped and ran barefoot all the way to the police station."

I tried to process what she was saying.
The police station was on the other side of town.
That was so far away.

She showed me her feet, which were bloody, and raw, with gravel stuck deep in her flesh and dried blood forming along the outside of her pinky toe.

"They didn't believe me. They told me that a husband couldn't rape his wife."

Her spine seemed to compress under the weight of it all.

"They told me that what happened, didn't happen."

The next night I was again sleeping in my brother's twin size bed with my mom. Jonny had burgundy colored sheets and a mahogany wooden bed frame. We had pushed the entire bed in front of the door to keep Dad out. Sometime, in the middle of the night, a huge thud rocked the bed. Like an earthquake, but inside the house. I was sleeping but jarred awake from the bed rocking as if we were on a ship in the middle of sudden swells. I lay there for half a second, frozen with fear. Dad was yelling on the other side of Jonny's door and mom started to scream. Rubbing my eyes to make sure I wasn't having a nightmare, I realized Dad was ramming his body against the door, trying to break in. He finally succeeded, knocking the whole bed over with a crash, spilling my mom and me onto the floor. In the dark, he began beating her senseless. All I could see in the dim light was a flicker of my mom's pink foam curlers beneath the huge shadow of my dad on top of her. His arm was moving forcefully and fast. I was power-less to protect her.

No matter what happened at night, the following days reeked of an enforced normality: we went to school, Dad went to work, Mom drove us to and from orchestra, ballet and swim lessons. They were friendly with other couples and hosted parties, espe-cially for the Opera Guild. When my parents threw parties for the guild my dad would offer everyone wine and drinks. He was incredibly proud of his wine cellar in our basement, and loved to discuss the details of fine wines with anyone who'd listen, or pretend to listen. Even me.

I always wondered if he enjoyed the elitism more than the alcohol, and if he'd ever be as delighted with me as he was with those crushed grapes. I remember standing outside the kitchen doorway before one of these parties, listening to my dad's voice as I stared down at my shiny black Mary Janes. "It's a common misconception that all wines improve with age," he said, "in fact, more than ninety percent of all wines should be consumed within one year. See, you swirl the wine around the circumference of the glass so that it absorbs more oxygen." He looked at me with the same intensity in his eyes as when he gave us spontaneous pop quizzes by making us add up the restaurant bill and divide it to determine how much it cost to feed each one of us. The wine in the glass he was holding was a deep blood red, it reminded me of swishing my mouth out with water when I got my tonsils removed the year before. But it also reminded me of the color in the bath-room sink as my mom washed her bloody face after my dad back-handed her and split her cheek open in the dark of Jonny's room.

I don't ever recall seeing my mom with a drink in her hand, although I know she drank. Some of those times involved pills and toxic combinations of the two. Both of my parents exhibited all the common signs of being alcoholics; there were stomach-aches and unexplained nausea, they were irritable and agitated and prone to big displays of emotion. Many times, I would come home from school and find my mom on the tile floor in the bathroom, sobbing in a fetal position. Looking back, it's difficult to discern which signs could be attributed to the dynamics of domestic abuse and those of alcohol abuse.

At the end of my first week of fifth grade I opened the back door after school. The air conditioner was on and it was cool in the house, especially for the end of August. Even so, my forehead broke out in a sweat and my stomach churned. Something wasn't right.

I braced myself and began to walk through the house. I passed through the living room but didn't see Heather, our Scottish terrier, anywhere. I paused, glancing over at our kitchen, with its dark cabinets and burgundy colored tile counter, but all I saw were bowls from breakfast, with soggy cornflakes clinging to the sides. Dirty dishes were fairly normal, unless my dad had just raged. Then everything was spotless.

I poked my head into the dining room, where we only truly 'dined' for Passover or other special occasions. I passed our breakfast table covered in a heavy red and white checkered plastic tablecloth, but saw nothing out of the ordinary. I started down the hallway, and paused at the basement door, afraid to open it, but did anyway. I peered down the dark stairs, and heard a sound. My back stiffened. It sounded like someone moaning.

I whipped around; the sound wasn't coming from the basement, it was coming from the piano room. My mom was lying on the brown leather sofa, her eyes rolled back into her head. She had vomit at the sides of her mouth.

"Oh my God, Mom!" I shouted. I heaved her on her side so she didn't choke on her vomit. It was another thing a nine year old really shouldn't know, but at that moment, I was glad I had learned. I grabbed a big mixing bowl from the kitchen, and put it on the floor beneath her head, then raced back to the kitchen and called 911.

My fingers were shaking as I dialed those three numbers I'd called so many times before.

"911 please state your emergency," the woman dispatcher calmly said.

"Please send an ambulance immediately, my mom is unconscious!" my voice cracked and I noticed I was panting into the phone.

"Okay okay, stay calm, what's your address?"

"565 N. Minnesota Ave."

She heaved a huge sigh, the verbal equivalent of an eye-roll, as if I was distracting her from her real work.

"Uh-huh." she said in an annoyed tone, "what's the problem now?"

"My mom is Unconscious!" I said, "Please send an ambulance, I don't know what else to do."

"All right." She sighed again, as if she was giving me one more chance to behave myself.

The cops had been called to our house many times. It seemed to take forever for the ambulance to get there. I tried to keep Mom on her side and the puke bowl beneath her mouth, I decided I'd worry about the cream-colored carpet later. Mom's head was heavy as I tried to hold it up; her perfectly wavy red hair was matted down with sweat and looked like she'd been rolling her head back and forth on the sofa.

She moaned again, her eyelids fluttering, showing the whites of her eyes.

"Mom, Mom, it's gonna be okay," I said. I didn't believe my own words but I hoped she did.

When the ambulance finally arrived, I explained the sequence of events to one of the EMTs, while the other one took vitals from my barely-conscious mom. Then they stepped aside and talked in low voices, too low for me to make out what they were saying. I started to worry that maybe it was much more serious than I thought. Trembling with the notion that these could be my last moments with her, I rushed to sit on the floor next to my mom.

The two EMTs came back over to me and loomed above a large, amoeba-shaped puke puddle on the carpet. Immediately I sensed their disgust. I was confused, why weren't they rushing her off to the hospital? They never asked me when my dad or siblings would be home and they never offered to call a friend or neighbor to help us. They just checked her vital signs, shrugged and said "She'll be fine." Then they left. What I didn't know was that to them, she was just a drunk woman with a hysterical kid.

A half hour later my mom was breathing a bit better. I scrubbed the carpet with a cleanser that stung the inside of my nostrils. Eventually I was able to help her into a bath so she could get cleaned up. She slept and woke up later that night with only a vague recollection that the EMTs had ever been there. It was yet another silent agreement between us not to tell what had really happened. She didn't have to ask me to keep her secret, I just did.

CHAPTER 4

"Ok Lisa," the Director said, "Now just sit on your heels, wearing an expression of pure excitement! Like, you just can't wait until your father comes home!"

"My dad?" I asked weakly.

"Well, yes, in this story, you can't wait for your father..." The Director paused, "You know, you're really excited to see your dad." She looked at me a bit more closely. I wondered if she saw terror on my face. "Or it could be anyone." she said quickly. "Just imagine, you're really happy to see, whoever you'd be glad to see!"

I glanced over at my mom, who was chatting with another singer. I wished she'd stop and help me, but she didn't. I was on my own, so I faked it. I tried to imagine I was a character in one of the many books I loved reading, losing myself in a magical story, one where the daughter is excited to see her father. The stories that were furthest away from my life felt like the best ones to read. But deep down, there was a thirst in me to read about someone who's life was like mine.

I was five years old and in my first opera, Madame Butterfly. The Omaha Opera Company needed a kid actor. I was an easy choice since my mom was the soprano and I was her youngest. I went from my half-day of kindergarten to opera rehearsals every day. I felt cooler and older than my kindergarten counterparts! The director was an uptight woman with a clipboard. In this scene, my character was required to sit back on her heels, while waiting for her beloved father to return home. For my first acting lesson, I wore my favorite denim overalls, shoving my hands into the wide sides and resting them on my soft belly. The director looked down at me as she tapped her pen against her clipboard. I could tell she didn't have or want to have children. Looking blankly at her, I tried to connect with the idea that a kid could be giddy with excitement for her father to come home.

The truth was that whenever I thought about my father coming home all I could feel was scared. Hearing the engine of his royal blue Fiat rev as it pulled into the driveway every night felt like a gnarled tree trunk in my gut. We never knew what mood he'd be in, so every time I heard his car I would unconsciously scan my room:

> *Toys – put away*
> *Bed – made*
> *Clothes – hung in the closet*
> *Shoes – lined up*

I knew that if any of these things were out of place, my mom would get a beating. And even if the night passed calmly, a week later he would whip out a single detail, a crime one of us had committed that had been carefully filed in the safety deposit box of his memory, and he would lash out at my mom. That's why I had to be a tracker, a detective hot on my father's trail so that I wouldn't miss anything, any details that might save my mother's life.

The idea of escaping my story began to consume me when I was five years old. I could just run away, like Jonny was known to do. He ran away on a weekly basis, mostly to the nearby creek, but one time he made it as far as Peoria, eleven miles away. I didn't like the idea of being out on the streets, but when your home feels like it is less safe than the streets, it's time to flee.

As soon as I began to read books without effort, I discovered that I could escape into a story. The moment my eyes met the page, I was instantly transported. I could become Meg in *A Wind in The Door* or Davey in Judy Blume's, *Tiger Eyes*.

Even talking to myself, telling myself stories, just going on and on, until...

"Lisa!" My mom would yell in her booming operatic voice, standing right in front of me. "It's great that you're so involved in reading, but have you fed the fish yet?"

"Oh God Mom!"

"Don't say G-o-d!"

"Ok. Geez Mom. Fish will be fine if he doesn't eat for another week. He's so huge."

Our fish's name was officially, "Fish" and he was the seventh goldfish we'd had in about five months. I wondered if Fish could hear the fights, or at least feel his fish bowl shaking from the impact of thrown objects or fists. Although Dad and the four of us kids were completely ambivalent about these fish, our mom would talk to them, and sing to them, just as she did the plants. But they kept dying too.

"It's your turn to feed the fish." my mom insisted, "And tell him you love him."

I looked at her to see if she was joking, but she was completely serious. So, I rolled my eyes, set down my book and went to find the fish food.

I didn't realize it at the time, but much like Fish, I became a big fan of food. About the same time, I began escaping through books, I also discovered the wonderland of sugar. And sugar was even better than books because I got a buzzy feeling after just a few bites. My friend Sally and I would walk the few blocks to 7–11 or Ben Franklin's and for twenty five cents we'd get two big fist-fuls of penny candy, little bite-sized snickers, sweet-tarts, choco-late balls and my favorite, laugh-y taffy! Not only was it flavored taffy—yum—but you got a free joke inside each wrapper. The jokes, like, "How do you get an alien baby to sleep? You rocket" were all cornier than the ones my grandpa loved to tell, but I always believed the best joke was still to come so I tore through those waxy corners searching for it.

Even more thrilling, was sneaking cereal boxes into the bath-room so I could eat, while perched on the toilet, all the marsh-mallows out of the Lucky Charms. Then, I'd hide the boxes in creative ways, like under a pile of clothes, or behind the pipes from the sink, or flatten the boxes out and place them under towels. I became a sugar junky, celebrating the ways I'd select my drug of choice, shoveling handfuls of sweet crunchy goodness into my mouth, letting the rush of sugar push me back on my bed, making me mind go numb, a smile sliding across my comatose face, I felt Free!

One of the ways my mom escaped was through her work. She had a number of different jobs like, selling kitchen knives door to door. Unlike me, she was comfortable talking with anyone. Then she began writing a weekly column for the Tazewell Courier, our local newspaper. I remember her driving me home from my violin lesson and suddenly pulling over to the side of the road, leaning over to search around in her bag and grab a pencil and a sugar packet upon which she began to furiously write, illegibly squeezing her words onto the tiny paper.

What I didn't see at the time was that on those disposable and mundane surfaces, my mom was brave enough to write about topics such as cruelty and war. Those seedlings were the essence of her weekly columns in the somewhat conservative Courier.

She wrote:

"I feel that there are rules for fighting, just as there are rules to follow in sports...Maudlin cruelty should not be necessary to defend one's position. When there is no other choice than to fight, when one's hard-earned freedoms and privileges will be lost if not defended, then fight with clarity of mind and with emotions in control. I, myself, certainly would not advocate sitting back and facing destruction... because I dislike war. But think of how many lives that would be spared...if words could be fired instead of bullets. And realize how many problems of the world could be eradicated by pen and ink. Bloodstained turf is not for me... nor do I want to visit my offspring as headstones lining a countryside cemetery. If ever I went to war... my ammunition, ideally, would be my pen... and my artillery, my ingenuity. If the following Biblical admonition ever comes to pass... perhaps we will be spared the further anguish of bloodshed and the loss of lives: They shall beat their swords into plowshares, and their spears into pruning-hooks; nation shall not lift up sword against nation, neither shall they learn war anymore."

Mom would write on anything: napkins, junk mail, deposit slips from her checkbook. And she put all these notes in her backpack. I was so embarrassed that my mom carried a backpack and not a purse like all the other moms. Whenever I'd whine to her, she'd reply with a wide grin, "this Is my purse. It's just bigger."

When her backpack got too full, she'd empty the contents into the wooden hutch that took up an entire wall in our formal dining room. The bottom of the hutch had four compartments with engraved wooden doors on them; each had a little keyhole. Many times, she'd lock her backpack in the hutch and I knew that she kept the key hidden, not from us kids, but from Dad. She guarded her backpack with her life; it was as if her writing was more sacred to her than her own body. My mom wasn't inherently secretive, she just got really good at leaving things out. I learned from her that there is power in locking things up; there is power in not telling.

One day she let me in on one of her biggest secrets; we were going to a new house. All she told me was that it was in Peoria and she would take me there to see it, but that I couldn't tell any of the other kids or my friends, and we absolutely could NOT let Dad know. There was fear in her eyes when she said it. We already had a house of our own, so I wasn't sure why mom had gotten another house. Peoria seemed a long way away, but Mom said it really wasn't that far. "Peoria, it's just the next city over, and it's bigger," she said, "and it's safer."

The first and last time I visited the house was in the fall of 1983. Velour sweat suits, belted blazers and polyester bow blouses were all the rage. Not that I cared that much about fashion, I was a few months shy of eleven years old and lived in sweatpants or overalls that I wore over my pink ballet leotards so I could play outside all the way up until mom dragged me off to ballet class. I hated ballet class. All the other girls my age were skinny as twigs, effortlessly bouncing through the air like they were born half kangaroo. I, on the other hand, with my thick thighs and chubby cheeks, felt like I was half wombat. My brother and sisters loved to tease me, pointing at the creases on my arms just above my elbows. "Stop picking on her!" Mom would say to them, then turning to me, "It's just baby fat, Honey, you'll outgrow it." I believed her, so when she asked me to keep her special secret, I did. It made me feel important.

It felt like it took forever to get to Peoria. On the drive, Mom seemed really distracted and excited at the same time. "We aren't moving here right away" she said, "we'll just be here occasionally, and then maybe someday we'll move in."

The new house in Peoria was small, much smaller than our home in Morton. Walking in the front door, you could see the living area, the kitchen, and a tiny hallway leading to a bathroom and two bedrooms. It was nearly unfurnished except for a card table and milk crates which acted like a dining room table and a big bed crammed into the slightly larger of the two bedrooms.

When we arrived, Mom asked me to go to the 7-Eleven just down the street, to see if they had nails so she could finish hanging pictures. I felt super grown up walking to 7-Eleven by myself with a five-dollar bill in my pocket. The door to the store was really heavy but a man with black skin and frizzy hair looking at magazines saw me tugging at the door and opened it from the inside. I stared at him for a second; we didn't have any black people in Morton. I said "thank you" and walked inside, touching the money in my pocket to remind myself that I was on a grownup errand. I started looking for nails. There was so much stuff, so many different packages that I couldn't tell which ones might have nails inside of 'em. All I knew was where the candy was. All of a sudden, I felt less grownup than moments before and tears started streaming down my chubby cheeks. How could I go back without any nails? I had failed.

So, I walked the three blocks back to the new house, wiping tears off my face, and even before I walked through the unfamiliar front door, my sixth sense which had been well-developed, was tingling. Inside, I noticed Mom's velour zip up sweatshirt was hanging off the metal window crank in the living room.

Immediately I had a funny feeling in the center of my chest like I was somewhere I shouldn't be. Years later, I would learn that this intuition, this sense of knowing that something is wrong, even before you have proof, is a protective skill common among children of trauma.

No one was there when I entered the living room. I scanned the room to see if everything else was in order.

Carpet - thick, dark shade of pumpkin, no signs of vomit
Walls - enormous mustard colored flowers, yucky wallpaper, but no signs of blood
Mom - nowhere to be found. I left the living room and went to the kitchen!

I began to walk into the kitchen, my heart pounding.

"Oh, Adam!" I heard my mother's voice say. Then I heard her giggling. I listened for a long minute as her laughter spilled down the hall. Was that my mom? As if she heard my thoughts, she came out of the bedroom, "Honey," she said, gesturing over one shoulder "you remember Rabbi Levin from Synagogue, don't you?"

It was a casual statement more than a serious question. The man who walked out behind her was completely average looking. He was a little taller than my mom, with short dark hair, a five-o'clock shadow, a prominent nose and dishwater colored eyes. His hands were in the pockets of his jeans and he was wearing a worn grey t-shirt.

But why was the Rabbi HERE? Was he going to bless the house? And why isn't he wearing his Rabbi outfit with the robes and all that?

Both my mom and the Rabbi stood there looking at me as if there wasn't a question in the world. I felt yucky. It was the same feeling I had when I got caught looking at the Playboy magazine my dad kept in his bedside dresser. I stared back at my mom and the Rabbi, "They didn't have any nails." I said, looking down at the thick, pumpkin carpet.

"It's ok, sweetie," my mom said, "we'll just get them at the hardware store."

I didn't know how my mom found the money to rent the house and I didn't know then that my mom and the Rabbi were having an affair. I didn't know that I would learn about adultery and rape before I understood sex and intimacy. I didn't know what made her fall in love with the spiritual leader of the temple we attended. I didn't know it'd take a few decades for me to have compassion for my mom and her choices. I also didn't know that my dad was sleeping with his secretary or that he would find out about my mom's affair and the rental house and that I would never go there again. I didn't know that my dad would out the Rabbi to his whole congregation and then threaten to kill him, running him out of town and all the way to Florida.

I did know that any time things didn't go the way my father wanted, he would assign blame to anyone but himself, and then crush them.

I knew that my mom was eccentric. Sometimes I'd catch her doing weird breath work. I thought it had been part of her opera singing training but they were yogic breath practices called Pranayama. Even though my mom never took a formal Yoga class, she was always practicing; long before yoga was something hip. I suppose she learned everything from the book I had taken to school for Show and Tell after the disaster with the diseased lung. Mom's large, hardback picture book about yoga featured a brown skinny guy wearing something that looked like a diaper, and his body was contorted into various poses. She kept it locked in the bottom cabinet of the china hutch in our dining room with other things that were precious to her. Things I was sure, if my dad got his hands on them, would be used as weapons against my mother. I knew that the sound of my mom laughing, was a sound I loved, and one I never heard often enough.

I knew that in the 70's Mom began to research electromagnetic fields and the effect of the neighborhood power towers on nearby human beings. Running seemed to calm her down, so she would go for a "run" by jogging up and down the long hallway in our house, holding on to her fairly large sized breasts as she jogged. It must've been before sports bras, but we made fun of her all the same. Mom also had a lot of costumes, including a gigantic rabbit suit that zipped up the front. She wore it around the house, and felt perfectly fine answering the front door while wearing it. She wore costumes like other moms wore regular clothing; sweat suits or dresses or jeans or skirts. She never talked about why she wore costumes, never called attention to it. She would casually sit on the large recliner in the living room, making macramé plant holders with one of her large bunny ears sometimes flopped over.

Maybe being a bunny or a Beefeater was better than being Mary. Better than being married to my father. Maybe she wore costumes to hide. Maybe that's why, sometimes, we pretended to be the Partridge Family.

Almost everyone in our family played a musical instrument.

I played the violin. Dad played the saxophone, Robin the viola, and Jonny played the cello. Mom's instrument was her voice. Sue didn't play an instrument, but the rest of us pretended to be the Partridge family. Music ran through our Fierer veins. It was the way we communicated with each other. It was an outlet for self-expression and a way to distract us. It was the glue that kept us together. Music created an illusion that helped us see past the constant fighting, insults and abuse.

We loved to sing and dance to The Elephant Song. My mom would usually start us off playing the piano, then we'd put our hands together, arms stretched above our heads, leaning over and walking around pretending to be Elephants, swinging our outstretched arm-trunks. Little did I know that thirty years later, I'd be teaching "elephant arms" in my yoga classes in reverence to the Elephant Deity, Ganesh. Ganesh, I later learned, is believed to be the Lord of Obstacles and Hindus typically pray to him before starting any new endeavor or project to remove any blockages to achievement. Ganesh clears the obstacles and paves the way for us to move forward in life.

Had I known, I would've invoked Ganesh in January of 1984. According to court documents, that's when my dad filed for divorce in Peoria County Circuit Court. Three months later, in May, my mom countersued for divorce. One evening in mid-May, 1984, my dad came home late from work, looking for a reason to be pissed off. We were just sitting down to dinner, Robin, Jonny, Mom, Dad and me, when my dad reached over to Jonny and grabbed him by the scruff of the neck, as if he were a puppy or a ragdoll. He yanked him up and out of his chair, dragging him towards the kitchen garbage can, which apparently, Jonny had forgotten to empty.

"Do you See the problem?" he said, his voice thick and sharp as glacial ice. Jonny didn't answer; he just picked up the can and took it out to the curb. When he came back in, Dad wasn't finished. He exploded out of his chair, dragging Jonny by his skinny arm into the living room, over to his science project, a chicken egg incubator, Jonny's pride and joy. "Is This the only thing that's important to you?" he hissed.

Jonny still said nothing. Dad shoved Jonny up against the wall as he reached into the incubator. He grabbed an egg and hurled it across the room at my thirteen year old brother. A high-pitched gurgling sound escaped Jonny's throat. My stomach turned as I saw the distinct form of a baby chicken fetus smeared on my brother's face.

"Now how important is the garbage to you?" Dad screamed. Jonny let out a deep mournful sob, and tried to run, but my Dad caught him around the neck with one hand, while smashing two of the three remaining eggs in his other fist.

In that moment, rage overtook my body, as if I'd suddenly burst into flames. I was powerless, but the anger inside of me was the size of Texas. I jumped up and pounded my dad's back as he punched and strangled Jonny. My mom and Robin were both there, but I was so focused I don't know if they too tried to stop him. In that moment, I made a pact with myself that someday I would be bigger, stronger and tougher than my dad; tougher than anyone – so that I'd never again have to feel that helpless fear and rage.

I didn't know it then but this was the beginning of a lifelong quest for physical toughness that would eventually lead me to bodybuilding, working construction, driving a big motorcycle and a one-ton truck. It was the beginning of my need for armor, through muscles and motors and men.

My mom filed a report on Jonny's beating and a Temporary Restraining Order was issued against Dad. A month later a Temporary Injunction was issued against both of my parents, but in June Dad violated the Injunction one night by breaking down her (Jonny's) locked bedroom door and taking her clothes and shoes. The police report mentions me: that I tried to stop him and he pushed me hard, injuring my hand. My dad was found in contempt of court and sentenced to 6 months of Probation.

The heat of summer was just beginning to extend past sunset, that night in June when mom flung open the window of my bedroom. "Get Herman!" she commanded me as she ran into my room, with her beloved backpack in her arms. I grabbed my favorite stuffed animal, Herman. "Jonny!" she shouted as he came running in. Mom began fumbling with the screen from the window behind the bunk beds. I could hear Dad's heavy footsteps barreling down the hallway as mom jumped out my window, over the tall shrubs. She was motioning for Jonny and me to jump too, but the ground looked so far. Mom held out her arms and I closed my eyes as my feet left the windowsill, getting scraped from the bushes as I landed, just barely clearing them. Jonny was right behind me, I could see Dad coming into my room as Jonny jumped. There was a police car parked outside our house, on the corner of Minnesota and Polk. I thought, maybe this time they'll protect us. But no one got out of the police car, so we just grabbed our things and ran towards it.

I didn't look back. Maybe I would have if I'd known that was the last time I'd ever set foot inside of 565 N. Minnesota Ave. That was the last time I'd see the place we called home.

CHAPTER 5

I never imagined that I would be living out of a station wagon that smelled like chicken, but that's what happened.

Mom was surprisingly calm as she drove Jonny and me to a small motel. *Maybe she'd been dreaming of this moment her whole married life.* The "Vacancy" light flickered in the motel office's window, beckoning us to come in as she hit the brakes. "I'm sorry you two," Mom turned to face us, "we don't really have money for a room."

Instead of going inside, Mom moved the wagon to the furthest corner of the motel's parking lot, away from the blinking light. We slept in the car. As my eyelids heavied, the last thing my eyes registered was the way the dim vacancy light highlighted lines on Mom's face I'd never seen before. Jonny stretched out on the backseat and I sprawled out in the far back. I clutched Herman to my chest, soaking the top of his fuzzy brown head with my quiet tears. I woke a few times during the night, startled by everything: the sound of passing cars, crickets, the wind. Each time I jolted awake, I saw Mom sitting upright in the driver's seat. She wasn't sleeping. Just sitting perfectly still, looking out the window, like a security guard scanning the area for intruders.

What happened to our small house in Peoria? Where was the rabbi? Why weren't we there instead of in a motel parking lot sleeping in our car? If I ever knew, I can't remember. I'm sorry.

One day, not long before we escaped out my bedroom window, Mom called Ethie's mom. My mom worked for Ethie's dad at the newspaper office. And Ethie was one of my best friends. They lived just a stone's throw away from our house. With her bright red hair and freckles, Ethie looked more like my mom than any of the four of us. She said my mom sounded "really weird," so Ethie didn't hang up when her mom got on the line. She heard the beginning of their conversation, and heard my mom talking about my father's violence, that this time he had shoved Jonny hard up against a wall. I don't know what Ethie's mom said to my mom, or perhaps, like me, she didn't know what to say or what to do.

I don't remember if my mom would have considered herself friend's with Ethie's mom. I don't remember my mom spending time with or really having any friends. But then again, with four kids, a few odd jobs, and an overly controlling husband, I doubt she had time for friends. I'm certain my dad did his best to keep her from connecting with others, and from asking for help.

Jonny had grabbed what remained of his cherished science project: his handcrafted incubator that held the one remaining egg that my dad hadn't destroyed. I don't know how the egg survived the events of that evening, but two days after we'd escaped, little chunks of shell began to fall to the incubator floor. It was 2:30pm on a Thursday; Mom had just pulled up to get Jonny and me from school. We all heard the shell cracking. Jonny and I leaned over the backseat to peer into the incubator. A patch of gooey yellow poked out of the cracked shell. Then, the crack spread upwards, threatening to expose the rest of the yellow goo. "Oh my gosh!" I screamed. Mom smiled, big. Jonny's eyes were wide. A tiny beak broke through the top of the egg, "It's Zipping!" Jonny hollered. The remainder of the shell fell away and, after a second of silence, it began chirping.

Where were Sue and Robin when we fled to the motel? Sue was nearly eighteen, and Robin was sixteen. I don't know if or how often I saw them during the next six months. They both stayed with our dad but I don't know if their staying was by choice or by default. I don't know if any decision at that time was made by choice or default.

For a few weeks, Mom, Jonny and I moved back and forth between staying in the motel and sleeping in the wagon. And then we landed. We finally moved from the faux wood-paneled station wagon into a house with white trim that Mom rented on the opposite side of town. As an eleven-year-old, that felt like the distance between Rhode Island and Montana, but I was just relieved to be sleeping in a house rather than in the car.

Our new house was a blue split-level with an unfinished base-ment about a mile away from my middle school. We didn't have any furnishings except for a card table and 4 folding chairs that served as our dining room table and bean bag chairs for a sofa. Our beds for the first four months were canvas army cots with wooden frames.

"Ok, let's cast votes for the first furniture we buy when I've saved up enough money," Mom sang cheerily. Jonny and I both shouted at the same time, "Beds, Couch, TV!" as though he and I had planned our response for that very moment.

Mom smiled. The same smile she had when she added a homey touch to our surroundings, like a huge vase with dried flowers by the front door or long, living room curtains that she sewed herself.

For more than a month, I was startled awake every time the phone rang, which was every single night at 2 a.m., 3 a.m. and a few times around 4 a.m.

One morning, while Jonny and I sat on folding chairs at a folding table eating breakfast, I asked Mom, "Who the heck is calling every night?"

Before she could answer I added, "Is it someone looking for the people who lived here before us?" Mom just rubbed her bleary eyes and said softly, "Don't worry, it'll be okay."

I was in tune with the cycles of tension and proceeding violence that erupted in our home on Minnesota Avenue, but was certain they'd stop when we left the confines of my father.

I didn't know the statistics at eleven years old. There was no way of predicting that after leaving their abuser, an intimate partner or spouse is at 85% greater risk of being killed by their spouse. All I knew was that the phone wouldn't stop ringing.

Fall was making its brisk presence known the morning Mom went out to warm up our car and take us to school. Within a matter of a few seconds, Mom ran back into our rental house, as if she had seen a ghost, slammed the door behind her and slid down the inside of the front door into a crumpled puddle on the floor. With our spoons full of oatmeal hanging in mid-air, Jonny's eyes met mine. "Mom?" we both said softly. Jonny pressed his hands into the tablecloth to anchor himself as he got up from the wobbly card table. Mom had sewn a tablecloth to cover up the instability of the table, a whimsical pattern that had rolling hills filled with apple trees, a bright red barn in the background, a smiling scarecrow in front, even a fluffy dog bounding through the piles of golden colored leaves. I was still staring at the table-cloth when I heard Jonny sit down on the floor next to Mom and say, "Would you like a glass of water?"

I got up and sat on the other side of Mom. She shook her head, looked at both of us, and smiled the kind of smile that let us know that her love for us would get her through this day.

Mom wrapped an arm around Jonny and the other arm around me. We sat there hugging on the floor for a moment and then Mom, as if a bolt of lightning hit her, hoisted all three of us up. She wiped the mascara puddle from under her eyes with her index finger. "The tires on my 'hot rod' were slashed. Let's start walking you both to school."

Mom lived in a constant state of anxiety: trying to provide for us, trying to keep our lives as kids fairly normal, trying to finalize the divorce with my Dad, and whatever else she had on her mind. We had some moments of reprieve, especially when we found Snuggles a calico kitty. Snuggles quickly became the high-light of our days; both Jonny and I would race home from school to play with her. She was butterscotch colored, the same color as our mom's '78 Mustang that she cherished.

It was shortly after we had moved into the rental house across town that Mom traded in the faux wood-paneled station wagon for what she affectionately called her, 'hot-rod'. Even though they were essentially both 'used', to us it seemed like we had both a new home and a new car. They represented the light at the end of a very dark tunnel. A glimmer of hope.

In early November 1984, Mom was able to obtain a restraining order against my dad and their divorce was granted but the formal order had not yet been filed. I wouldn't know that for years to come.

I did know we planned to have Thanksgiving dinner at the Open Bible Church in Hopedale, the only place where my mom seemed to really light up and relax. We'd been going to this Church with our mom for over a year. I didn't feel quite comfortable at the Bible Study classes nor at the big services, but I could tell Mom felt really supported by the people there, so I kept my mouth shut. They all knew her name and hugged us when we came in. Thanksgiving really was a test in holding my tongue; instead of a nice big table with a huge white tablecloth and candles, the church put out a buffet. It felt more like a homeless soup kitchen. I sulked, wishing we could, for once, have a normal Thanksgiving dinner, without anyone throwing food or punches.

Just a few days after Thanksgiving we celebrated my twelfth birthday – Jonny, Mom and me. Even though we ate cake off paper plates and my presents were small, I knew things would get better now that Mom had left Dad and they were getting divorced. Mom was trying to make it special for me, but she was very distracted.

"Mom, hey Mom!" Jonny called to her across the large space between the living room and the kitchen. We could both see her in the kitchen and wondered why the heck she wasn't hearing us. Right after Thanksgiving, Jonny and I found the perfect spot in the new house for the Christmas tree that we couldn't wait to get. Jonny and I plotted that we'd ask Mom on my birthday, if we hadn't gotten it by then, both sure that she couldn't deny such a request on my birthday.

Jonny shot me a look in the silence of Mom not responding, that prompted both of us to see what she was up to. She was just standing there in the kitchen, holding a dish towel, staring out the window. I took his unspoken cue and, since I was about five feet closer to her yelled, "MOoooooooM!"

She jumped and turned towards us.

"What Honey? I'm right here!"

"We, Jonny and me, would really like to get a tree and put it right there in the corner on the wall with the fireplace. Won't that look awesome?" I said.

She smiled softly, "It's 'Jonny and I', that's the proper grammatical usage. A good way to check if you're unsure is to try half of it. For example, 'me would really like to get a tree.' That sounds silly doesn't it, so you can deduce that 'I' would be correct grammar." I always appreciated how gently and consistently she would teach us. A far cry from our dad's methodology.

"Kids, we all really want a tree and it's on the top of my list to purchase..." as her voice trailed off, I could tell she was stressed. She rarely, if ever, called us 'kids'. Jonny and I got the hint that she was doing her best to manage more things than we could begin to understand. "We'll just have to see how it goes, ok?"

Three days after my birthday, December 6th, 1984, Mom woke us up early. The way her eyelids drooped signaled she hadn't slept much the night before. It was the morning of the day she was supposed to divide furniture with our dad at our old house. She was worried about seeing him for the first time since the night of our escape.

Once my parents began the divorce process, the four of us were appointed a "Guardian Ad Litem" named Jim Brandy who was supposed to supervise everything to make sure our interests were represented. But to us, he was just some guy appointed by the court, to oversee the division of furniture as movers loaded it up and moved it to our new house so we wouldn't have to eat Lucky Charms on a card table any more.

I don't recall ever meeting this Brandy guy. I'm pretty sure I would've remembered meeting someone with his physicality: he was 6'7. But I wouldn't learn that for about thirty years.

I remember noticing that Mom's usually steady and clear voice was hesitant and scratchy that morning. I wondered if she was really scared. It was more of a fleeting thought, most likely followed by some thoughts about what my day would be like or what we'd be doing after school. I loved to come home after school and indulge in a big bowl of ice cream with chocolate syrup before Mom got home from work. I remember walking out the door that morning going to school, knowing I would see her when I got home that afternoon.

CHAPTER 6

The loudspeaker in my social studies class announced, "Lisa Fierer, please come to the principal's office." Everyone in class turned to look at me. The roomful of eyeballs on me made me realize I was the one whose name had just been called. I glanced over at Mr. Durham for permission to leave and he nodded his head at me. I shrugged my shoulders towards the class, trying to play it cool.

I headed down the long hallway catching glimpses of my face, which appeared distorted in the polished linoleum floor. As a good-hearted troublemaker, I typically knew my infraction before I arrived at the Principals' office. Like when I rearranged the letters on the Morton Jr. High School sign-board so that it said 'Turdsay' instead of Thursday? But tus time, I mean, this time, I couldn't identify what violation I was getting busted for.

Nervously, I peeked my head around the corner where Mrs. Mason, the principal's secretary sat. Rather than wearing her traditionally stern expression, she looked sad when she saw me, and had tears welling up in the corners of her eyes. I couldn't stop myself from biting my short fingernails as she escorted me into Principal Johnson's office. As I rounded the corner I saw Mr. Johnson standing between two police officers. The officers in navy blue uniforms towered above him—way above me—one by at least six inches and the other nearly a foot taller.

All three were shifting their weight back and forth, almost rocking. None of them looked at me, which was weird, because I was the only one there. Mr. Johnson glanced at me for a second and then quickly looked away, as if looking for an escape route.

The taller of the two officers kept fidgeting, adjusting the leather holster on his belt. No one seemed interested in telling me why I had been summoned. I tried to make eye contact with the shorter officer, who was looking the most solid of the bunch. I caught his eye. He swallowed; I watched his large Adam's apple slide down his throat. He said, "Lisa, we need you to come with us."

It was only five blocks from the Jr. High to Lansing's house on the corner of Illinois St. and Sunset Rd. But time dragged and the silence in the car was thick. *But why were we at the Lansings? Bob Lansing was Sue's boyfriend, and his sister Lucy was my best friend, but why were we here, ringing their doorbell after an awkward car ride with the two silent officers? Why was I on my best behavior, curling my hand in my lap like I was posing for an Olan Mills school portrait?*

The shorter officer rang Lansing's doorbell. *That seemed so strange to me,* I thought, *I always just walked in.* Sometimes I was with Lucy, but even when it was just me, I'd open the front door, peer through the screen door, then just go in. If it was after 4 p.m., Mr. Lansing was usually home from his job at Caterpillar, and super glued to his lazy boy chair in front of the TV. Occasionally he would grunt hello at me from his chair if he saw me coming in. Then I would give a little wave as I ran upstairs to see if Lucy was in her room so we could play. If I didn't find her there, I would head to the kitchen. I loved hanging out at the Lansing's: they always had junk food, unlike our house. Occasionally we'd have Lucky Charms or Captain Crunch cereal, but they had Doritos, Oreos, and always, multiple flavors of ice cream. I didn't consider ice cream junk food- it was a staple, the fourth food group left off the food pyramid we learned about in Health Class.

Jonny, Robin and Sue were all sitting in Lansing's living room, along with Mr. and Mrs. Lansing. Everyone seemed to be pretending this wasn't odd, including the two officers who stood awkwardly in the Lansing's entranceway. The taller one was rubbing the inner sole of one of his overly polished black shoes against the other. The shorter one began,

" We're terribly sorry to have to tell you this," he began wringing his hands.

"Something awful has happened with your mom and dad and your mother is no longer with us."

What? There was a ringing in my ears. His words swirled around my ear canal but nothing went in. *Did he say my mom was no longer with us? Did she escape somewhere? Could he mean that she's dead?*

Dead? I don't know if that word formed in my mind or in my mouth. Like a foreign language I was just beginning to learn, the meaning was just out of my grasp.

He took a gulp of air as he said the next line, "And your dad is in the hospital."

I tried to barricade his words from getting into my brain. It felt as though I'd just been transported inside a novel where the story takes a wrong turn and I'm stuck inside the wrong turn, inside the wrong story. I could see Robin crumple, and Jonny's jaw tighten as tears rolled down his face. My sister Sue turned and ran downstairs saying, "I'm not surprised! This was bound to happen!"

I stood there, in front of my siblings, flanked by officers, not understanding any of it. *Mom no longer... Dad in hospital...*Like I was trapped in a bubble, some other reality where cogent sentences said are translated into gobbledygook without your permission. The cops seemed anxious to run out of the house after their announcement. "We're so sorry to have to tell you this news...."

This steel-toed boot of news about my mother dying was like a sucker punch to my gut. Instead of blood gushing from the impact of the punch, tears flowed. I couldn't stop them, they just kept coming, waves obscuring my vision, washing away my thinking. The only thought I was acutely aware of was how much I wanted to be comforted by my mom. I had just turned twelve years old and all I wanted was comfort from the one person who was now, forever, gone. My mom. No longer.

And then the flood of wondering. Who would be there to hug me before bed and to clean up my milkshake mess? *God, I promise to not leave the ice cream out to melt all over the counter if you can bring my mom back. You can bring my mom back, can't you?* Who was going to tell me stories and wrap me in warm blankets when it's cold?

Mom was by far the best storyteller. From the time I was four until eight, she hosted a Children's Story Hour at the public library. She was a one-woman Foley studio, making all kinds of sounds to enhance a story, to create tension; she'd raise her voice to convey excitement and then bring it down to a whisper, making all of us lean in to listen intently. As her daughter, it made me instantly cool and I loved it.

At the moment when the officers announced that Mom was dead, I had been appalled at what Sue said before she left, but it was true. I wasn't surprised, either. I had known for a long, long time that my mom wouldn't be here. I thought back to all of the notes she wrote to me: slipped into my launch box, tucked into my pants' pockets, that I saved. The sweet words scribbled on napkins, lunch bags, pieces of colored paper, even one on a sugar packet. Every note, I squirreled away into a small cardboard box that I hid in my dresser drawer. I knew it wasn't normal for a kid to do that, but I had to, it was inexorable.

What about Christmas? My mind continued to spin. Since Thanksgiving I'd been nagging Mom about getting our Christmas tree, especially since we could have one this year without worrying about Dad tearing it down. Jonny and I had moved the tan, metal folding chairs and black bean bag chairs that we called our living room, over to one side, clearing an enormous space designated as "The Christmas Tree Area." Even though it wasn't a special space, just a bunch of shag orange and brown well-worn carpeting, I kept picturing the six foot spruce that would soon be standing there in all of its glory. That was over a week ago. Every time Mom looked at that space, I saw sadness in her eyes. I wondered if we'd even be able to afford a real tree that year.

The cop's voice came back to me "your dad's in the hospital." What the hell happened? Where was my dad – did he do This? The taste of bile came up the back of my throat like the time I smelled the diseased lung Dad made me take to school.

Over the next week no one said anything about my father. When I asked, I was simply told that he was in the hospital. And then they gave me the pat answer: We're investigating. Why couldn't the cops just tell us what happened? I thought of their motto, the one inscribed on the side of police vehicles "to serve and protect". So why weren't they serving me? Why couldn't they protect my mom? What kind of jackass makes a promise they can't keep and then prints it on their car?

I knew they knew more than they were letting on and I would continue to be furious with cops in general for years to come. At that moment, when I had essentially lost both of my parents, the police were the easy and uncomplicated target; one I desperately needed. If they had done a better job, or followed the paper trail of times they'd been called to "Fierer family residence", maybe this wouldn't have happened.

I thought about the time my dad had raped my mom while we were at Sunday school and she had run barefoot all the way to the police station where they turned her away; denying her desperate plea for help, and denying the reality of what was happening in our home. *Serve and protect WHO?*

My head was spinning. I just wanted to go home, crawl in my bed and cry with my teddy bear, Herman. But I was told that I couldn't go home, both the house on Minnesota Ave and the house Mom, Jonny and I lived in were sequestered. And still no one told me why.

The transcript from my father's trial, which took decades to access and read, is the only record we have of what happened, or might have happened, that morning at our family's house on Minnesota Ave. According to the testimony that was eventually given at the trial, my mother and father mutually agreed to meet at our family home for the purpose of dividing up their belongings. Jim Brandy, our guardian ad litem, was at the house, as well as two workers from a moving company. Around 10:30 a.m. my dad said that my mom went home for about forty minutes to get boxes and came back, but that she refused to take off her coat. My father said that he went into the kitchen to get a garbage bag to put things in. Brady went to make a call on the kitchen telephone and then he "heard a commotion" coming from one of the bedrooms, followed by a woman's voice screaming for help. When he went to the bedroom, Jonny's room, he saw my father on top of my mother in the doorway of a closet. He said that my father's arms "were moving rapidly and there was blood on the wall of the closet". Brandy, at close to 7 feet tall, attempted to pull my father away, but was unable to do so. He then took a record carrying case and hit my father in the head with some force, but "even that blow elicited no reaction". So, Brandy ran from the house seeking help and the two movers went into the bedroom. One attempted to pull my father off by the belt and shoulders, but was unable to move him. The other mover found a baseball bat and used it to strike my father on the collarbone. The blow had little effect.

By the time the first police officers arrived, my father was laying on the floor on top of my mother's body. He "did not respond to verbal orders and had to be carried to the hallway". When medical personnel arrived, he was placed in an ambulance. The technicians "applied various forms of painful stimuli, attempting to elicit a reaction" from him, but he did not respond. One of the technicians described him as "disoriented" and testified that his eyes did not react normally to light.

My father testified that he and my mom had gone into the bedroom to sort items of property. He went into the kitchen for a garbage bag and when he returned he knelt down next to my mom, who was kneeling in the closet. He said that the next thing he noticed was "a knife coming at him". The last thing he remembered was grabbing the knife by the blade and trying to wrestle it away from her.

My father did have knife wounds on his hands about which the two lawyers argued. Were they offensive wounds or defensive ones? An expert for the defense described the wounds as defensive, while the State's witness testified that they were more likely to have been caused by slippage of the defendant's hand from the handle onto the blade of the knife. My mother died from the resulting loss of blood after suffering twenty seven stab wounds. Twenty seven stab wounds. I'm not sure what there is to argue about with twenty seven stab wounds.

CHAPTER 7

The headline on the front page of the newspaper the next day said "Local Doctor in Hospital, Wife Dead."

The newspapers were one of the only ways I learned clues as to what had happened to my mom. The Lansings got the paper delivered daily; I could hear it 'thwunk' as it landed on the concrete of their front porch. But when I'd come downstairs, it was nowhere to be found. Four days after my mom died, Mrs. Lansing asked me, "Do you want to read the papers?" Her voice was soft. I was thankful for her straightforward question.

"Thanks for asking," I told her, "it's weird, but I think I do want to read them. Just to find out what's going on."

I'd lost track of what day it was. The paper read Monday, December 10, 1984.

I don't know who authored her obituary:

"MARY FIERER
Mary Ellen Ruth Fierer, 45, of Morton, died Thursday,
Dec. 6, 1984, of stab wounds at her former residence,
565 N. Minnesota St. She was born Feb. 11, 1939, in
Dunkirk, N.Y., to John H. and Mildred C. Fox Bailey.
She married Dr. Joshua Fierer June 14, 1959, in New York
City. Their divorce had been finalized at the time of her
death, according to court records. Surviving are
her ex-husband; four (typo), Sueela, Robin and Lisa, all
of Morton; one son, Jonathan Fierer, of Morton; and her
in-laws, Mr. and Mrs. Norman Fierer of Brooklyn,

N.Y. Her parents preceded her in death.

A 1961 graduate of Brooklyn College in Brooklyn, N.Y., she was active in the Peoria Youth Symphony. She was an advertising saleswoman at Tazewell Publishing Co. in Morton and attended Open Bible Church in Hopedale. Private funeral services were scheduled for Monday. Visitation was also private. Burial will be in Mennonite Cemetery in Hopedale, the Rev. Brad Hunt, of Open Bible Church officiating. Ludwig-Rohrschneider Mortuary in Morton is in charge of arrangements."

Private funeral services were scheduled for Monday. Visitation was also private. Burial will be in Mennonite Cemetery in Hopedale, the Rev. Brad Hunt, of Open Bible Church officiating. Ludwig-Rohrschneider Mortuary in Morton is in charge of arrangements."

My father was hospitalized at St. Francis Medical Center, under guard by the Tazewell County Sheriff's Department. The newspaper said he had extensive cuts on his hands and was undergoing surgery on them. The house at 565 N. Minnesota as well as our rental house were still part of a crime scene and both houses were sealed during the investigation. When you watch cop shows on TV, crime scenes seem mysterious and accessible. But in real life, when your home is a 'crime scene' it means that all of your toys and possessions, everything you own at both Dad's and Mom's house are unreachable. Even clothes. When I learned that I'd have to borrow a black dress to wear to my mother's funeral, I locked myself in the upstairs bathroom at the Lansings.

The funeral was in Morton on a cold, overcast Monday. The room itself seemed foggy, with shapeless people entering the space then disappearing into the corners. It was lit like a stage set, with my mom's casket in the middle of the stage under a glaring spotlight with everything else, everybody else, in the shadows.

I know that my siblings must have been at the funeral, as well as people my mom knew from church or her job at the paper. But I was in shock and felt so alone that I have no recollection of who was there. It was just me. And my mom in a casket. Even after all these years, that's still such a strange phrase to me: my mom in a casket.

I was virtually frozen until my violin teacher Arthur began to play. Somehow the music thawed me and my tears began to fall. Fast. The music allowed me to finally feel the loss of her. I remembered the times she would drive me to my violin lessons, just us in the car driving towards music, had been some of the best times I had with her. Even with a pond of my own tears, I began to have an unquenchable thirst.

Someone, for unknown and unfathomable reasons, had decided that my mom should be in a half-open casket. They dressed her in a white frilly turtleneck shirt to hide the knife wounds on her neck and chest. I wondered how many hours the make-up person at Rohrschneiders had to spend smoothing over the cuts, making her murder disappear. The truth was that the body in the casket didn't seem like my mom at all; it seemed fake, like a wax rendition of her instead of the person I was closest to in the world.

With the exception of my mom's funeral, the days, weeks and even months that followed her murder are inaccessible in my memory, like another black hole preventing the light from escaping.

The papers informed me that on Jan 7, 1985 my father was

ordered to stand trial and denied bond, but on Jan 8th there was an arraignment hearing. *In case you're wondering, as I was, what the hell an arraignment hearing is: it's a court proceeding in which a criminal defendant is formally advised of the charges being placed against him and is asked to enter a plea in response to the charges.* My dad pleaded innocent and was released on $30,000 bond.

Years later I'd learn that my mom had apparently made her will when she was first married, leaving all her property and assets to my dad. And due to a technicality, their divorce was not finalized by Dec 6th when she died. So, he fought in the courts to inherit all of her assets, the sale of which he used to pay his legal bills. My father's first trial was delayed twice and finally held on Oct 6, 1985.

I had never seen my dad cry, not once, not ever, until the day I visited him in the county jail. He was sitting across from me, on the other side of the Plexiglas wall, wearing an orange Tazewell County Jail jumpsuit. As he looked at me, the tears were rolling down his face, but even then, even through the scratched Plexiglas, there appeared to be a disconnect between me and the reason why he was crying.

I pressed the phone receiver as close to my ear as I could get it and watched a tear slide from his left eye, over his cheekbone and hit the rocky terrain of his five o'clock shadow. "Fleabop, it's so difficult in here," I held my breath waiting for him to say he loved me and how sorry he was.

I waited.

I squeezed my eyes shut, trying to will the sounds I wanted to hear come through the tiny holes in the receiver.

Nothing.

Instead of empathy or regret for his uncontrollable rage, he was crying for himself.

The only sorry he felt was for himself.

I opened my eyes.

The faintest smirk hid in the corner of my dad's mouth and behind his eyes. My belly felt like it was on fire. I realized he wasn't crying for what he'd done. The heat rose to my throat. Those tears were for himself. Because he was behind bars. There were no tears, no remorse for the fact that he had imprisoned his entire family.

CHAPTER 8

I don't know what made me throw that first dish, but it felt really good.

For six months after my mom died, I was a foster child of Betty Housen and her biological daughter, Candice. Every day that I awoke in their guest bedroom, the mismatched green curtains and light blue walls were in silent cahoots, signaling to me I didn't belong there. It wasn't and would never be my home. Don't get me wrong, I was relieved to be living indoors and with people who weren't exactly strangers. Candice had been best friends with Robin in high school. Even though they were best friends, they fought a lot. During one of those fights, Candice mailed Robin a random square she cut out of Robin's sleeping bag. I never learned what, if anything, Robin had done. Just a few days later, they were making plans for the weekend as if nothing had happened.

No one witnessed me flinging the dish. The faded red flowers in the dish pattern cascaded in uneven chunks down the wall of my bedroom. Leftover bits of butternut squash hanging on for dear life. It felt so good to chuck the plate that I hurled my coffee mug against the wall too. I was slightly disappointed that only the handle broke off, so I picked it up and chucked it again. Destroying the dishes elicited a rush in me that made me feel like a delinquent superhero. And then I had a thought, *I wonder if this was the kind of powerful rush my dad enjoyed when he punched Mom and smacked my brother around...am I just like him?* My stomach felt like it did when I got food poisoning from some bad fish tacos at

Coney Island. I slid down the wall and hugged my knees into my chest; the butternut squash was now clinging to my hair, I was a mess.

My heart pounded like a giant fist on the door of my rib cage. What would Betty Housen say?

She was like nearly everyone in Morton, Illinois, living by the unofficial slogan, 'let's make everything look good on the outside!' Despite the fact that underneath the surface of her little red Corvette and perfectly coiffed hair, lurked a basement, literally, and in that basement, were a bunch of cats (11) and a full bar.

I guessed she was sitting silently in the kitchen or in her bedroom across the narrow hall from "my" room, the guest room they had given me to use. I imagined her ear pressed against my bedroom door, her diamond hoop earring pushed to the side as she listened. And I anticipated a lot of silent scorn over breakfast in the morning.

What I really needed was a platter the size of a house, something big enough to throw at everyone so they would stop walking on eggshells and start talking about my mom's death. I desperately wanted someone who would allow me to simply be broken. And then, slowly pick up each piece; inspect it with loving hands to patiently assemble the jagged edges of myself back together. Every time I heard the story of Humpty Dumpty, it was like a mouthful of three-month-old milk. My greatest fear was just that: that no amount of aid could put me back together.

It seemed like everyone in the entire state of Illinois knew how my mom had died and it became harder and harder to do the simple normal stuff that teenage girls do. So, when my sister Robin invited me to go shopping with her one day I jumped at the chance. It had been just over a year since our mom died and

I realized this was the first time I'd spent time alone with Robin.

It was early August 1986, Robin needed clothes for her freshman year at Illinois State University. I found it funny that she was going to college in a place called Normal, Illinois, since our lives were anything but. She offered to pick me up at the Housen's. I was touched that she thought of me and how I'd need new clothes for my freshman year at Morton High School. While I loved shopping, I'd already begun to hate my body. It didn't help that Candice and her mom (the cat hoarder) both taunted me about it.

"Rob!" I yelled from across the hip store in Northwoods Mall "I'm gonna try on this shirt, K?" She glared back at me with her index finger pressed vertically across her lips. The universal sign for 'shhhh'.

In a split second my excitement turned to shame.

Why was I always doing stuff that annoyed and embarrassed her?

I took the teal wrap around shirt into the dressing room.

The dressing cubicle was big and well lit, with beige carpet, beige walls and a swinging door that latched from inside. There was a two foot gap of open space at the bottom of the cubicle door.

It had taken me forty five minutes to find one top to try on, while Robin had already purchased four full outfits. I loved every single piece of clothing in that store. But in a split second, I'd think, "that's so cute, but it'll look awful on me." Or, "I'll make those nice pants look like a cow jumped in them."

As I fumbled the shirt off its hanger, I heard Robin say, "Lis, hurry up!"

I could just picture her waiting at the dressing room entrance with her hands on her hips, tapping her foot.

I decided to leave the wrap tied to make things quick. I barely had begun to get the shirt over my head when I found myself stuck in the fabric, unable to tell where the armholes and head hole were. I fought with the fabric, but was losing as Robin continued to stage whisper, "Lis!"

In the midst of getting swallowed in the shirt with no foreseeable way out, my bladder let me know I had to pee. Now.

I struggled with a bit more determination, only getting more frustrated and frantic. All I could think was, *I have to go, I have to go!*

I began laughing at the absurdity of the situation when I heard,

"Lisa Renee, Hurry Up! Geez!" Robin must have heard me laughing, and assumed I was having a great time while making her wait.

Mid-laugh, I heard a ghastly sound:

Phhhhhhhhhhhhhttttt

I had laughed out an enormous fart.

As if I'd just dosed myself in laughing gas, I was now in hysterics, flailing my arms above my head, still entombed by the damn wrap-trap shirt. Just then my bladder burst.

Warm liquid poured down my legs, soaking my jeans. Without the ability to see anything, thanks to the shirt shielding my sight, I relaxed for a moment in the sheer relief of my body getting to do what it so desperately had needed at that moment.

Robin began banging on the door.

"Lisa, what the hell are you doing in there?"

I stopped laughing long enough to whisper, "Rob, I'm stuck in this shirt and I peed myself. "

She gasped.

"Oh my God, you What?"

The fact that she was appalled and I was still stuck, initiated a new round of laughter.

Between snorts of giggling, I said, "Can you get me some toilet paper?"

Less than thirty seconds later, Robin crawled under the dressing door with a fistful of paper towels.

"God help me if I get your pee on me while I'm crawling underneath, I'll kick you."

With Robin's exasperated help, I did escape the wrap around shirt and shuffled out of the dressing room in an attempt to hide the large pee stain on the front of my pants. Twenty minutes later we were driving back to the Housen's and Robin's frustration with me had dissipated.

It would take me years to see that I was just a little kid who was literally trying to hold way too much inside and failing miserably. It's a wonder my body didn't combust into flames. At that moment, I was stuck in clothing and I simply couldn't contain everything that was being held inside.

When Candice Housen wasn't looking, I'd stare at her legs. Her whole body, really. She looked like a model; for all I knew, she may have done some modeling. Her legs were so long and lean, her skin permanently glowed the color of cinnamon toast. Sometimes I'd close my eyes and smell her just to see if she smelled like fresh-baked cinnamon rolls. She didn't, but if I could have chosen to look like anyone, it would have been her. She was perma-glow and I was more perma-pudginess; a condition I couldn't seem to shake. My thighs were too thick, I was too short, my mom was dead. Not a winning combination in Morton (or anywhere else, for that matter). I did lose five pounds in the couple of weeks that Betty Housen convinced me to take brisk walks with her every evening after dinner. But then there was the occasional batch of brownies Betty would make and leave to cool on the counter. Those brownies were chocolate sirens, sending their lustful fog in my direction, luring me into the kitchen where I'd find myself slicing a quarter inch from the whole length of the pan, so it didn't look like I had taken another square. Damn those brownies.

I was bullied by more than just brownies. Sue was seven years older than me and she never let me forget it. To her and her friends, I must've appeared like a terrier always nipping at their heels. Like many older siblings, she seemed to guard her time and privacy with a vengeance, while insisting at every turn, that she never got the same attention and privileges that us 'other' kids got. Once she received her driver's license, she wielded it like a newly appointed police officer, flashing badge and pulling rank. I always tried to talk her into taking me out for ice cream, but Sue had stopped eating ice cream her freshman year at Purdue University. In fact, I think she stopped eating all together. When she came home for the holidays, she was half her previous weight. The jeans that fit my eleven year old body were swimming on her eighteen year old one. From August to December, her weight had gone from one hundred sixty pounds to eighty five pounds. I was scared and confused and spent a lot of time eavesdropping on heated discussions between her and Mom and Dad.

About ten minutes after I began tossing dishware at the Housen's walls, the phone rang and I heard Sue's voice say "Hey, Lis how are you?"

I began to weep.

"What?" she said, "What's wrong?"

Between sobs I managed to squeak out, "They call me 'fatty fatty two by four, can't fit through the kitchen door.' I know they think they're just being funny but it's so mean. I'll never be skinny like them but they don't have to make fun of me."

I accidentally inhaled my bottom lip making a loud, slurpy sob sound.

Sue's voice got really loud, "I am coming right over and taking you out of that place. There is no reason you should have to deal with this after everything we've been through."

My mind was still swimming in circles when Sue and her big pregnant belly burst through the Housen's front door. Counting the months on my fingers, I figured out she must have gotten pregnant about a month before our mom died. Sue was all business as she began to toss all my belongings in bags. I was sobbing as I tried to pick up the pieces of the coffee mug I had thrown against the wall. Sue hissed, "Leave it. They can pick it up. We just need to go." She was like an angry momma bear doing whatever it took to protect her cub.

We didn't talk in the car. Sue seemed to be simultaneously restoring her energy for whatever may be coming next, and also, lost in thought. Now she not only had her life and the life of her soon-to-be-born baby to plan, but suddenly she had another unexpected child to plan for: Me. I think that was the closest I've ever felt to her; at that moment, she was so clearly doing everything necessary to protect me, when she was in such a vulnerable state herself.

Once again, I was swept out of a home, not knowing I would never return there again.

What I missed most at the Housen's was the full-size bar they had in the basement. Once I shooed the cats off of it, I was enamored with the array of bottles; the size and shapes of glasses, like snowflakes, each one unique, perched on shelves and backlit with tiny lights. And a full mirror covering the wall behind them, showing their glory twice. The more I stared at them, the more I became transfixed.

I'd have Lucy Lansing over to the house and at first, the long swigs we'd choke down felt a lot like I imagined chugging gasoline; burning the inside of my throat. But the burn was worth it because it always gave way to a tingling sensation that filled every inch of my chubby body. The tingles were my ticket to boarding a liquid flight to destination: 'anywhere but here'. Lucy and I would take a few swigs from a number of bottles and fill the missing portion with water; an age-old trick that, apparently, is not as clever as we thought. The jackhammering I awoke to in my head was never enough to dissuade me.

It was 1985 and my father was entering the first of what would become two, multimillion dollar trials. I knew enough to know that the burden of proof is on the Prosecution, and that the Prosecution was supposed to be advocating on behalf of my mom. I also knew that my father's side, the Defense, aimed to plant the notion of "Reasonable Doubt" although I didn't know how that could apply. No one was debating the fact that my mom died of twenty seven stab wounds at the hands of my father. I wondered what there was to determine.

At twelve years old, I was deemed too young to testify and too young to be in the courtroom. It was absurd that strangers were trying to shield me from what I had experienced my entire life. Finally, there was an opportunity for me to tell everyone what had happened behind closed doors, to shed light on the violence that had become normalized. I wanted to testify. No one had ever shielded me from the harm at home. And no one had protected my mother.

As it turned out, none of the four kids testified. There had been questions raised as to whether the 'older siblings' should testify on behalf of my dad, the defense or on behalf of our now dead mom, the prosecution. The determination, I presume by the costly defense team my father and his parents hired, was that since there was only one parent left, we should have the opportunity to be parented by our father. What-the-actual-fuck?! When they told me that it was better to be parented by a violent murderer than no one, I couldn't stand it. To have my experience completely dismissed was enough to make me want to explode. Enough to make me want to jump on the backs of the defense team and try to make them stop hitting my mom.

The trial was the most publicized 'secret' Morton had ever witnessed. Walking down the hallway at Morton Jr. High, I'd pass kids who didn't know me B.M.M. (before my mom's murder) and their conversations would abruptly stop as I walked by, some sneaking a sideways glance at me. The kids I did know began to wear an expression they may have learned from their parents. I interpreted it as, 'you are different from us'. In my lower moments, it felt more like, 'you're a freak'. I'd later learn, it was pity.

I quickly began to notice that exceptions were being made for me. During Physical Education class, I just laid on the gymnasium floor while my classmates ran laps and paired up for wheel barrel races. P.E. was an easy class for me to test out my budding rebellious personality. I'd failed it for a number of years prior, due my inability to do push-ups, pull-ups and the dreaded rope climb to pass the President's Test. Also, it was easy to place judgment on our P.E. teacher. She more closely resembled a pumpkin than a specimen of agility and strength. I didn't really want to disrespect her, I just wanted to be treated like a normal kid, to be expected to do everything that other kids were doing. All the adults were so freaked out by mom's murder that no one wanted to talk with me. Adults didn't know what to say so they just stayed away from me, when all I needed was someone to talk to. I desperately needed someone to talk to.

In the summer of 1985 Lucy Lansing invited me to go with her to a carnival in Peoria. As gregarious as I was, Lucy was shy. She kept her kiwi green eyes hidden beneath her thick curly blond bangs. The carnival had everything teenagers love: cotton candy, swarms of boys trying to be cool, and spinning cup rides. At the same time, Lucy and I spotted a sign, "Your Life Revealed to You, Palm Readings $3.00"

"Oh my god, a Psychic! We should Totally do this!" she said.

"Fine," I said, "but you go first."

The carnival psychic was wearing a purple flowing skirt, with rings on each of her fingers, and long purple painted nails that she used to motion for us to sit on the velour cushions in front of her. She gestured for Lucy to follow her behind a curtain, into the back of the tent for her "reading".

Lucy didn't seem too impressed when she re-emerged, but she was a tough read; Lucy had a perfect poker face. She flopped down on the cushions, as I apprehensively followed psychic-lady behind the curtain. I wasn't the least bit surprised to see a large crystal glass ball.

"Have you ever seen a psychic before?" she said in a throaty voice.

I looked at her like, *seriously, you're asking someone my age that question? I just started menstruating, I'm just a kid.* I always swung between thinking I was the most mature twelve year old ever and playing the kid card.

I shook my head no.

"First, I look at your palm." I stuck out both palms like I was about to get handcuffed.

Is she faking a German accent?

She took my right hand and turned it palm up. Her fingers were surprisingly cold.

Maybe she's cold blooded, like a snake, I thought.

Her eyebrows shot straight up her forehead as she fingered my palm.

She traced the line that stretched horizontally across the center of my right palm; then closed my hand quickly. Holding my fist, she said in a thick maybe-real-maybe-fake German accent, "you have experienced such difficulty...your parents..."

She was just getting started, but I quickly pulled my fist out of her grasp and held it close to my belly. Scooting out of the wooden folding chair I said, "Ok. I'm done. Thank you."

I nearly ran past Lucy on my way out the tent. She caught up with me. "What the hell happened in there?" she asked, catching her breath. "I hope it wasn't too bad, I paid for both of us."

I felt like I'd left my body.

"So... what happened?" Lucy's voice snapped me back.

I told her exactly what the psychic had said.

"Huhhh," Lucy replied. I felt like I was holding my breath under water, eyes squeezed shut and fingers plugging my nose. "Maybe she saw my picture in the Tazewell Times, and knew from that, that my dad murdered my mom," I said with my eyes closed.

"Maybe..." Lucy said slowly.

I silently vowed from that moment to keep both my palms

and my past locked deep inside. If I never told anyone what had happened in my family then hopefully they would never know.

CHAPTER 9

"Miss, Miss, did you lose something?" The Emma Willard School night guard called loudly, scaring the shit out me. I knew we had night guards, but this was my first real encounter with one. You could see them strolling through the shadows of the Victorian lamp posts, like extras in the film version of 'my so called high school life'.

I was shuffling through the leaves trying to find the condom, in its bright foil wrapper, that my friend Josie had tossed out the window to me.

"Um, yes. Sir." I paused. The piercing light from his foot-long industrial flashlight momentarily blinded me. "My favorite bracelet fell out the window." I told him, thinking and blinking rapidly, "I know it's supposed to snow tonight so I wanted to get it right away."

"Oh, well let me help you." He said, "You'll need a flashlight to look in the dark."

My heart was pounding, I couldn't tell whether he believed me or not. I suddenly realized he might actually shine his flashlight on the condom wrapper.

"Yay! I found it" I lied, reaching down and pretending I was putting it in my pocket for safe-keeping, "Thank you so much for your help," I gushed.

"Okay, go back inside. It's getting chilly."

It was late October 1987 in Troy, New York. I thought the guards were hired to protect the students from all the harms that lived outside of Emma Willard School. But they seemed to think they were parents in uniforms, intervening when we 'children' in the castle might be breaking the rules unbeknownst to the resident housemother in each wing.

Troy, NY housed Emma Willard School, the oldest all-girls' school in the nation, founded in 1821. It was steeped in academic and old English tradition, boasting an annual Mayday celebration, holiday season Madrigal-like play performance and some of the finest, well-educated females of the century.

It never felt like a fancy castle type school when I attended, but years later, watching the movies *Scent of a Woman and Emperor's Club*, both filmed on the grounds of Emma Willard, I could see the portrait of majestic stone buildings with cupolas, a bell tower over the library and the menacing stone gargoyles (watching our every move) and realized, yep, I went to school in a freaking castle.

Josie knew I was going to see Shawn at (RPI) Rensselaer Polytechnic Institute, the college nearby, when she chucked the condom out the window. Josie was a rebel with a laugh that sounded like wind chimes and a constant yeast infection that prompted her to shove yogurt up her vagina while easily maintaining a conversation with me at the same time. She hid a car off campus just in case we needed a getaway vehicle to see boys or drink alcohol. We stored several bottles of liquor in the trunk of her car. And she knew one of my secrets that I didn't even know: I blacked out when I drank, because I drank A Lot.

At fifteen years old, lies came as easily to me as breathing. Lying went hand in hand with recklessness, one of my best features and something my friends marveled at. In addition to lying, I cheated on most of my tests by writing answers on the bottom of my shoe or the inside of my pants. Especially in history. While I hated history, I was intrigued at the anomaly that was my history teacher, Mr. Betterly. He was a lanky six and a half feet tall, always wore plaid flannel shirts, hiking boots and had the longest legs I'd ever seen. His neck and wrists were adorned with Native American turquoise jewelry. As my appointed High School Advisor, Mr. Betterly quickly became my most favorite adult on campus. I wondered where he stored the endless energy and excitement that bounded from his bony body. He was the only teacher I ever told about my mom's murder.

I thought going to boarding school was going to be cool, like the TV popular show at the time 'Facts of Life'. I read in the brochure that this particular school was Jane Fonda's alma mater; not knowing at the time why that mattered, but hoping I would end up with a body like Jane Fonda's when I graduated.

My schoolmates and I did workouts in the hallways to Jane Fonda tapes. My favorite was "Start Up" because it was less time than all the other work-outs (only twenty five minutes) and pretty easy, even for someone as out of shape and uncoordinated as me. Despite Start Up, I graduated with an extra thirty pounds.

It must have been our 'tea time' meetings. That's what our resident assistant called our weekly dorm meetings. Perhaps during the time of Emma Willard's inception, teatime was a formal ritual, one meant to educate and refine young women's manners; our teatime, however, didn't involve tea at all. We made and ate pounds of raw cookie dough, occasionally accompanied by ice cream and treats received in care packages. Instead of the fancy tea dresses that the Willard ladies of yesteryear wore, we donned oversized boxer shorts and grungy tee shirts.

None of my friends at school knew the real story about my dad killing my mom. My roommate, Penelope, was the most persistent in her attempts to pry details from me about my life.

She was a combination of confidently nosey and totally insecure and desperate for friendship all wrapped in the thickest Alabama accent you could imagine. We became running partners, because that's what two chubby girls do when talking is tough. Plus, when you're huffing and puffing up a hill it's easy to avoid pointed questions.

"So... if it's okay to ask..." she paused as we ran up the hill on Elmgrove Avenue, just outside of campus. We began running downhill, "how did your mom pass away? I'm so sorry about it, and I just, well, I just want to know you better."

Her southern sweetness bothered me. But I had avoided this question for an entire year of being roommates. "She, um, she died of can-cer." I half choked on the lie and hoped that made it more believable – to myself more than Penelope. I was glad we were running beside each other so she couldn't see my eyes. I don't know if she believed me but it halted her incessant questions.

Penelope was plump, like the cookie dough I was so fond of. Her flesh protruded like chunks of chocolate chips trying to escape through her snug shirts. With her auburn hair and freckles, she reminded me of a heftier version of the Peanut's character: Peppermint Patty. Her outgoing nature broke through my initial shyness and apprehension at all the newness coming at me at Emma Willard. The only connection we shared seemed to be our love of eating and the struggle to get the numbers on the scale to decrease. Penelope turned me on to running and taught me how to breathe while running uphill and through those painful side cramps. Although I appreciated all of this, my Junior and Senior years I chose to room with Josie, Jaqueline, and a few others in a separate house on campus reserved for upper-class(wo)men.

As I was nearing graduation and feeling a certain dread that came to me whenever I found myself leaving home, never to return, I tried to distract myself by pretending to care about what all the other girls were obsessed about: losing weight before the ceremony, which dress to wear (we had to wear white dresses) and how to get a tan when it was still freezing cold May in upstate New York. But my secret obsession was, "how the hell am I going to deal with seeing my dad out of prison for the first time?" Our only family friends, the Channings, were coming to my graduation, along with my dad's parents. I was glad there were going to be a number of others to deflect the interactions between Dad and me. Beneath my immediate concern were the hot coals of rage that my father had only served less than six years of his twelve year prison sentence.

My main form of communication with my dad while I was in high school was through letters. I told him I couldn't accept any collect calls on the payphone because it was shared with seven other classmates in our dorm. But the truth was, I wanted to avoid having to explain to anyone why I'd need to receive a collect call from a state penitentiary in Illinois. I crafted a long, handwritten letter when I had an idea I wanted to share with him. By that point, I knew enough about my father that any idea would have to be one that appealed to what he loved, otherwise it would be null and void. My father was a sailor. With a belly full of vodka chugged while hiding beneath the lifted trunk of Josie's car, I proposed to him that a Summer Semester at Sea, living on a sailboat in the British Virgin Islands, would be the ideal way to embark upon my upcoming Freshman year at University of Miami in Coral Gables, FL pursuing a major in Marine Biology. To most kids my age, this would've sounded downright dreamy, but for me, it seemed like my only viable chance to avoid having to live with my father, soon to be a newly released convicted felon.

"Dad," I wrote, full of liquid courage, "you and I both know that kids who arrive well prepared for college, have the upper hand to success."

I never used phrases like, 'upper hand' and 'success' but I knew full well they'd appeal to my Ph.D. father.

"Flea-bop," he began, in his written response. I could see he was trying to wear me down using an outdated nickname, "it'd be so nice to have you here in Peoria with me for the summer. I have a nice apartment and I got an extra bedroom just for you."

I'd rather be mining for hot lava in hell, I thought, than spend the whole summer there with you.

Surprisingly, I won the what-to-do-the-summer-after-I-grad-uated-high-school-debate.

The morning of my high school graduation, early June 1990, started off chilly and hazy, typical for early summer in upstate New York. Unlike my classmates, I welcomed the grey sky and chilly air. There were seventy of us graduating in the splendor of Emma tradition: all in white dresses, white shoes, poised to sit on white folding chairs, lined perfectly against the backdrop of ivy covered stone buildings. My nerves were on guard, working over-time, scanning my body, the chairs, the audience, back to my body, the audience, the sky, the air, everything, everyone for a threat.

I had spent the last month before graduation bingeing on cookie dough and over-exercising to try to get the dough off my thighs. I wasn't alone; my friends Jen and Jenya along with a few of my boarding school mates joined me, each with their own version of insane pre-graduation dieting. On graduation day, I poured all one hundred and eighty four pounds of my 5ft. 4-inch self into my strapless white dress. The dress was embossed with textured white roses on the bodice and layers of gauzy white fabric on the bottom that would, hopefully, disguise my expanding hips. I felt like an embellished marshmallow.

My father arrived wearing a dark suit and grey hair that looked more like weeds begging to be pulled than the distinguished salt and pepper "do" I'm sure he hoped for. Although I hadn't seen him in person, we had spoken on the phone when he called his parent's house (my grandparents') when I was there for visits. I noticed from conversations, that he had picked up some fake prison-slang: "you can't con a con" and "that doesn't jive with me" as if he were in some bad prison movie. He told me he had been given the nickname "Doc" and boasted about earning a law degree while incarcerated. My mind flashed to the era when I was seven to ten years old and I'd see him watching the evening news, throwing remarks at the T.V. about criminals and "hard earned tax dollars being wasted on such trash."

He stood, along with my grandparents and the Channings, at the reception talking and joking easily, as if he had never been convicted of murder. As he funneled fistfuls of hor d'oeuvres into his large mouth, I hoped none of my friends noticed. I can't imagine any of my other classmates were as scared of their fathers, their futures as I was. The only thing I knew was that there was no way I would ever live with him again. Every time he began talking to me, I'd edge my way over to Alex or Aaron Channing or scan the room to see if I could catch the eye of one of my friends. They all seemed engrossed in enjoying their families and success.

I don't remember enjoying any moment of my graduation, only the feeling of sheer exhaustion at evading my father's conversations. All I wanted was an infinite amount of alcohol.

I was thrilled to step foot on the fifty foot Moorings boat in Tortola, BVI, that I and eight other newly graduated kids from all over the US (and even one from Sweden) would call home for the next two months. I had successfully appealed to my dad's love of boats and looked forward to discovering if I even liked them myself. Our rigorous schedule of scuba diving to earn Dive-Master Certification, along with daily sailing lessons and chores kept me active, engaged and far away from my dad. The work and on-the-go schedule was balanced by a few of us sneaking cigarettes and alcohol. It didn't take long for me to realize that I was more corrupt than all of my shipmates. It seemed I was motivated by something far greater than they were: *I had nothing to lose.* I had no place to go back to and lacked the understanding of home and what that meant, especially when my shipmate from Sweden would break out in tears missing her family and the familiarity of her culture. Not me!

I began to discover that traveling was a socially acceptable form of escaping. It was like finding a friend that wouldn't ask about my past, only care about where I was going! The vast water that we swam in daily was a deeper blue than any blue I had ever seen, like all the blues swimming together. This peaceful, azure galaxy that lived beneath the surface was an entire world for me to discover.

While scuba diving one day, I sat on fire coral and was sent to what was called 'a witch doctor' on Tortola."Turn, turn so your fiery behind is toward me," I'd come to love the sing-song way in which natives of the Caribbean spoke. "It'll be alright, just a bit of a sting." I hadn't gotten a good look at him, the pain made me squeeze my face, my eyes buried like spelunkers. The tingling in my rear was electric and the sensation made me think nothing of pulling the bottom of my swimsuit to the side like I did when I had to pee. "Just a little liquid to counter the effect of the coral." His voice was softer. My back was to him. I breathed deeply and my nostrils filled with the smell of whisky. Instantly, he poured it straight onto my ass. The intensity was searing like an army of fire ants attacking my derriere, and then it suddenly dissipated. Later I'd realize that was a magical moment; the marriage of my two loves: the ocean and alcohol. Yes!

After two months in paradise, I returned briefly to my dad's apartment in Peoria. Hardly a home, the jolt of being in his dilapidated apartment felt like the slam of steel doors entrapping me into the reality that was my life. With a bit of forethought, I had invited my friend Josie to come with me as a buffer between my dad and me. His apartment was a long dark hallway, with a kitchen plopped in the center, 1950's mustard-colored carpet and grey walls. Josie picked me up at the airport, recognizing me right away, even with my newly bleached blonde hair from the Caribbean sun and my skin the shade of darkly stained maple.

On the way to my dad's apartment I offhandedly said, "Being at my dad's might be a little awkward."

"How come?" she said, looking at me.

With the speed of an auctioneer I said, "Because he just got out of prison, he took my mom's life when I turned twelve and I haven't really hung out with him since he got back."

Josie went white, but kept driving. "Holy shit!" she hollered.

So much for the truth setting you free; I felt like I had just begun to dig my own grave.

This was the first time I had ever told any of my friends about my mom's death, and it would be a long—and dark—time before I did it again.

CHAPTER 10

Giving myself a black eye seemed like such a good idea at the time.

"Did you hear something?' I heard Sandy whisper.

I froze and waited.

"Probably just one of the guys." Paul replied.

"Now, what were we talking about?"

I could hear a smirk in Paul's voice.

Sandy kept her whisper voice, now more seductive than scared.

"Yes, I'd like to kiss you."

On the night of my failed-black-eye attempt I drank a six pack of Pabst, three White Russians and a few pina coladas. I was just getting started. Just before my vision got blurry, I had seen my mostly-ex-boyfriend Paul, and Sandy, another girl on the crew team, leaving the on-campus bar & grill, the Ratskeller, together. They ducked out quickly but I spotted them. Waiting a few minutes, I staggered swiftly toward Paul's apartment. Pausing at the entrance, in my alcohol clouded judgment thinking, I thought, *fuck him*, quickly turned the knob and let myself in. Breathing a sigh of relief that his roommates, all of whom were on the rowing team with us, were not in the living room, I walked down the hall. His bedroom door was locked. My anxiety was building, I heard voices in his room and pressed my ear against the door, just like I'd done as a child.

Like the bubbles beneath the vent of Old Faithful, I could feel myself about to blow. If the door hadn't been locked, I would have walked right in. The alcohol I'd ingested made me forget my paralyzing fear of heights, so I threw on an invisible cape and scaled the side of the three story building. Climbing the wrought iron railing on the outside of the apartment building, I maneuvered my way up to the third floor with American Ninja-like leaps fueled by the liquid courage I'd consumed. I pressed my face against the glass of the window to see exactly what-the-fuck was going on. They were in his bed together. I almost fell off the tiny ledge that barely held the width of my sideways turned feet. His window was open a crack. I stuck my fingers in to pry it open with one hand, my other hand held a ready fist.

"What the?!" Paul yelled bolting up in bed. I fired the cannon of my fist through the open window, hitting his front teeth and breaking one. Paul, not missing a beat, grabbed both my wrists and pulled me in through the window.

"Oh, now you have us both in your bed!" I shouted. "I bet that makes you happy!"

"How did you get up here? You are so drunk!" his clear green eyes were wide with disbelief. Even in a state of upset, Paul was calm. The opposite of me.

I couldn't stop myself from swinging punches and yelling. I'd begun to sob, which made my utterances indiscernible, even to me.

Paul took hold of my arms, with his 6ft. 6 frame, his arms seemed longer than my whole body. He began to walk me down the hallway and out the front door.

"You can't Do this!" I heard myself yelling. He locked the front door behind me.

I banged on the door, knocking off flakes of brown paint. Even in my drunken state, I could hear the hollowness of the door in the reverberations of my fist. Just as I began to wonder if I could punch my way through it, I noticed a pile of 2 x 4's just outside the front entrance. I grabbed one and ran down the stairs to look for Paul's car. I spotted Sandy's faded red Honda Civic first.

Just as well, I thought, and I began swinging the 2x4, coming down on the headlights, the windshield, then the sides and hood. My wrist was screaming in pain, but I was on a mission. *How dare she get into bed with Paul!*

I always wanted to study the sea and the underwater world of life that existed deep within it. I longed for the opposite of frigid upstate New York, so sun drenched Miami, Florida was perfect. I'd be close to the water and I knew I'd find an ocean of alcohol there. The University of Miami is in Coral Gables, just outside the notorious party place of South Beach. Palm trees lined the walkways of the sprawling campus, begging for hammocks to hang from their trunks. It was a far cry from the proper New England tight community of Emma Willard. Although I'd failed Physical Education classes throughout grade school, not for misbehaving and not for lack of trying, but for sheer lack of strength and coordination; I managed to receive a rowing scholarship.

Being on the crew team gave me a sense of purpose. I didn't even mind the random drug testing required for Varsity athletes or the fact those arbitrary testers always seemed to select the Rowers and Tennis Players rather than the Football Team. We met for practice at 5 a.m. in the predawn heat and our practice took us through the inlet, along rows of fancy waterfront houses. It beat the hell out of rowing on the cold water of the Hudson. Our Emma Willard crew team had once rowed past a mysterious floating shape and heard later, it was a dead body.

I loved being on the water, thinking about nothing else, focusing on the timing of the person in front of me and how my rowing oar pulled through the water. I liked the physical challenge, the feeling in my body, the burning in my lungs and that magical moment when all the small details came together into one seamless action. I loved that I was solitary while still being part of a team, all of us moving as one entity, cutting through the water.

The crew team had training rules, which meant that we could not drink while training for a race, called a regatta. There were random drug and alcohol tests for Varsity athletes to ensure we were abiding by these restrictions. My skewed perception of balance meant that I would not drink for weeks while training, race, then have an all-out drunken bash. I was frequently a 'happy drunk' rolling around on the floor laughing and often inadvertently mopping up any spilled liquor with my mane of curly blond hair, earning me the glamorous nickname, "Mop". On occasion, I became an angry and violent drunk; the scary thing was, I never knew which version of me the alcohol would unleash.

Exhausted, with my wrist throbbing, I dropped the 2x4 and sat down on the curb to admire my handy work. I didn't know yet that my wrist was broken, I only knew that it hurt. I could hear sirens in the distance and knew they were headed my way. Someone must have seen or heard me whacking Sandy's car.

Shit! I need a good story, and fast. *I know! I thought, I'll give myself a black eye and say that they beat me up because I caught him cheating.*

I tried hitting myself with my right fist first but my wrist was killing me, I just couldn't get enough force. So, I tried with my left, but that was pretty awkward.

So, I grabbed the 2x4 and lemme tell you, there's nothing like a good board and face whacking to help you sober up. After a few solid hits, I dropped to the ground, sobbing. Unfortunately, all the bashing only seemed to bring up the emotions I was trying so desperately to escape: devastation, depression and darkness. Panic kicked in. I was suddenly surrounded by cop cars- if only they had given me just a bit more time; I think I could've succeeded in the blackening of at least one of my eyes.

I don't know what the cops expected to find, but it probably wasn't a sobbing drunk girl pummeling herself in the face. They didn't quite realize that I was the one who had put the huge dents in Susan's car, and she wouldn't discover and report it until the next day. Later that night when I got back to my dorm room, I was still upset. My roommate was out. I went to take a shower and clean up, attempting to wash off more than just the blood and dirt. While I was in the shower I saw my hot pink daisy razor lying on the shelf. Suddenly it seemed like a reasonable idea to try and cut my wrist with it. I wasn't a cutter and I didn't really want to die but I knew, at some level, that I needed help. I just didn't know how to ask for it. I couldn't figure out how to extract the razor blade from the pink casing. Thankfully a plastic safety razor makes a pretty bad suicide tool and I was only able to give myself a shallow cut. When my roommate came home she took one look at me and called the paramedics.

In lieu of being arrested, I was placed on a disciplinary probation, and required to:

- Meet with a University Psychologist
- Meet with Head Crew Coach and the Assistant Head Coach
- Have absolutely no contact with Paul
- Have absolutely no contact with Sandy
- Create and adhere to a payment plan for repair of Sandy's vehicle

It didn't help that I had a cast on my wrist which got me suspended from the next three races and that my roommate was best friends with Paul since they were in first grade so she was constantly talking about him. Soaking in my own tears and misery, I'd illegally sit on the ledge outside our first-floor dorm room. Muttering to myself about all the injustices that were brought upon me, while alternating between taking drags of a Camel cigarette with one hand, and biting off fistfuls of Twizzlers with the other. It'd be years before I'd hear the line that I should've tattooed on my fists: "I'll show you, I'll hurt me."

The meeting with the University of Miami Psychologist was the worst.

I walked into his office ten minutes late and dropped into a chair, crossing my arms across my chest.

"Hello Lisa." He said politely.

"Mm hmm." I made the sounds from the bottom of my throat.

"How are you doing?"

I just stared at him.

I could tell he had an agenda, and he kept staring down at a pile of papers in front of him.

"What's that?" I demanded, looking at the folder resting on his desk.

"This is your family history."

"Are you fucking kidding me? How the hell did you get that?"

"I think we can offer you some help," he said in a faux sweet voice, dodging my anger.

"I don't need your help!" I leapt up, spun on my heels and slammed the door behind me.

It was like being at the carnival psychic's all over again. As much as I attempted to guard my family's history, it would always rear up. I felt as though the effort it took to "put the past behind me," a phrase my father was overly fond of saying, absolved me of any accountability or responsibility to answer any questions. As far as I was concerned I didn't have a problem with anger, violence or alcohol. I just wanted everyone to leave me the hell alone.

I phoned both of my sisters, embellishing just a bit about my role in the situation for which I was being punished. Sue was living in Champaign/Urbana, IL with her then husband, my 7 yr old niece Brooke, and my 5-year-old nephew, Darrell. Robin was living in Bloomington, IL and the two of them collaborated to come visit me in Miami over spring break. It wasn't until they arrived that I realized I was desperate for their company. Part of what I referred to as, 'my parole', included being confined to campus, which meant I had to miss a huge regatta in Tampa, Florida. Shortly after Robin and Sue arrived, I showed them around campus and the three of us went out dancing. We went to a club off the main strip in Coral Gables notorious for being lenient with underage drinking. In celebration of our first time out together as adults, Robin handed me a fluorescent blue colored icy drink as Sue shouted, "Oh my gosh! We have to go dance to this! It's Sister Sledge!" She grabbed our hands and pulled us to the center of the dance floor.

Alcohol, and the sheer bliss of being united again through music, aided us in avoiding any talk about our father. All I remember is the hot Miami air and crowd of body heat that melted the make-up we'd spent no less than two hours applying. We danced in our own triangle of wriggling hips and flowing arms. Occasionally we invited the nearest good-looking guys to join in. We were scream-singing at the top of our lungs, "We are Family! I got all my sisters with me!" The rest of the evening quickly became a blur. The next day, they helped me nurse a wicked hangover (I vowed never to drink blue drinks again).

Two and half months later, I transferred schools. My story at the time was that I got kicked out of the University of Miami. A notorious party school, people seemed astonished and I hoped, impressed, by what they presumed to be a wild exit. In hopes of finishing up my schooling at DePaul University, I moved in with Robin and her two roommates in Lincoln Park, Chicago. A place that was, unbeknownst to us at the time, soon to be the hippest part of the city. But my overwhelming thirst for oblivion and self-destruction was growing and Chicago was also about to become one of the most dangerous places of my life.

CHAPTER 11

"So, do you have any waitress experience?" the owner, Jared asked in my interview. I discreetly tried to rub my sweaty palms on the front of my black Gap pants. In spite of my nerves, I was focusing intently on what he was saying and trying to answer.

"Well not really, but I'm a fast learner," I stammered, "and a hard worker. I'm a hostess two nights a week at the pasta place down the street."

I couldn't stop looking at him. Just the way he shifted his hips on the stainless-steel barstool made my heart race. If I had a 'type', he was it: 6'4, eyes that changed color like moonstones depending on how much light was present, and strong hands that occasionally would move through his hair as he chose what to say next.

He wasn't really looking at me, instead looking all around the room, checking to make sure everyone in the diner was getting good service. Just then, the front door opened and a group of men in their 60's entered. "Hey Charlie, Jim! How are you guys?" Jared called cheerfully to the two in front as they headed toward what I learned was 'their table'. As Jared walked over to greet these 'regulars', he called over his shoulder at me, "Can you start on Monday?" It was more of a statement than a question and he didn't even meet my gaze. In that moment, I decided I was bound and determined to get him to like me. I mean, really like me.

In the Spring of 1992, I left the ocean, my scholarship and all my troubles behind. Or so I thought. I went to great lengths to get as far away as possible from University of Miami, and the mess I'd made there. That same year, when the leaves were clinging to the last vestiges of summer, I was clinging to the idea of a new start. I was accepted as a transfer student into DePaul University. DePaul was nestled in the soon to be up and coming Lincoln Park neighborhood of Chicago, just a stone's throw from the L Train. Since I could no longer bask beneath palm trees, I rode the L Train and listened to the wheel flanges of the Brown Line clanking on the rails, as if tapping out the fate of my future. I set my face in what I thought to be a 'city glare', tucked beneath the black US Rowing baseball cap I wore daily. The hat had never been through a wash cycle and if that wasn't a deterrent enough, I conjured the look of 'don't fuck with me' to deter any potential friendliness or passersby from saying, "Hello".

My attitude of apathy helped me ease into a space I'd call home, a nook even smaller than the tiny University of Miami dorm room I lived in the last two years. My sister Robin and her three roommates were gracious enough to let me squeeze into their two-and-a-half-bedroom apartment. At just under fifty square feet, the sunroom was considered a half bedroom: just barely big enough to hold a single size mattress and two milk crates. It was perched on the second floor of a two-flat facing Lill Street, less than a mile walk to my Sociology and Anthropology classes at DePaul.

Pets of any kind were forbidden to renters, but the landlady, our downstairs neighbor, Mrs. Andre, had four cats and a litter box smell that wafted through my bedroom vent and could rival my stinky US Rowing hat any day! Mrs. Andre looked strikingly like a squashed old lady version of the wrestler, Andre the Giant; the association making it easy for me to remember her name, a blessing since I'd never been good with names. Mrs. Andre didn't hide her fondness for my sister Robin; she'd leave her notes and tiny gifts of potted plants- overgrowths from her spider plants and ivy. I assumed the plants were trying to extend as far away from the cat stink as possible. Mrs. Andre's endearment towards Robin was the polar opposite of her disdain for me. Unlike Robin, I made it easy for Mrs. Andre to have contempt for me. Especially when I smuggled a ten-week-old Husky puppy into the apartment.

I was working as a hostess and aspiring waitress for a charming little Italian restaurant that was known for its hand crafted, cut-to-order pasta. The owner, Robert, a thin, hot-tempered chef with a mullet and a salient nose, shared the living space above the restaurant with two Siberian Huskies, Jade and Jasmine. I felt an immediate kinship with them. At thirty pounds over a healthy weight and a mane that poofed out beyond the width of my shoulders, I was pretty husky myself. Little did I know at the time, I'd have a string of love affairs with restaurant owners and Huskies. And although Huskies have reputations as runners, they'd stay in my life a lot longer than the restaurateurs.

It may have been a last-ditch attempt to incite Robert's affection, but when he told me about a husky puppy who needed a new home, I jumped at the opportunity. Robert drove me the 100-mile trek to and from Joliet, IL. My eyes met those husky blue eyes as soon as the door opened and he bounded right at me, all fur and roll-y pol-y awkwardness. Two hours later, I had him tucked into my sweatshirt and smuggled into my room. That was the extent of my plan. Robin found out about the illegal fur ball the same night he arrived. I left him for exactly thirteen minutes to take a shower. During that time, he managed to chew a hole in every single pair of my underwear and tossed all my belongings around my room as if a burglary had occurred. Lucky for me, and for Harley—my husky pup—Robin's a sucker for baby animals.

Three months later, when he'd outgrown smuggle-size, Harley and I moved into a slightly larger, yet far more dismal apartment half a mile away from Robin.

My employment at the Italian joint was short lived. I can't recall if I was asked to leave or left on my own accord. It may have had something to do with the Port and Frangelico I helped myself to every night from the bar. I shrugged it off; I was picking up more shifts at the diner where the 6'4 owner welcomed the regulars. Despite my inability to arrive on time (even though my apartment was only two blocks away) and getting pissed off at customers (like the day I 'accidentally' spilled chilli in the lap of a guy who shouted at me clear across the room), I hung onto this job. In three months, I managed to move up the ranks to better shifts without getting fired when the sexy owner announced we'd be having a staff celebration to commemorate the opening of a second diner.

The day of the staff party, Marty, the short order cook, doubled his intake of alcohol – he usually kept a fifth of vodka in his white cook's coat. Standing in the kitchen, I noticed that both pockets had matching red caps sticking out.

"Hey Marty, can I have a pull off one of those things in your pockets?" I half joked. I needed it just to calm my nerves and stop obsessing about what I was going to wear that evening.

"Sure," Marty said, narrowing his eyes at me and handing me a bottle.

A minute later, the owner's brother Jenkins came barreling through the kitchen door, the scent of last night's tequila still trailing behind him. Jenkins was a notorious drinker and drug user. Although I never witnessed it, I think he did cocaine and most likely dealt it. His work life was questionable and he typically only showed up at the diner when he was hungry, hung-over, or out of cash. Jenkins was nearly a foot shorter than Jared and, if you measured his width at the pinnacle of his beer belly, he was almost as wide as he was tall. Compared to Jared's full head of hair, through which he'd run his hands when he was deep in thought; Jenkins had patches of hair and bare scalp, as if a six year old with clippers had at it.

At the party that night, beer tequila and rum flowed freely as the staff, friends and family celebrated Jared's hard-earned success. I had decided to wear a jean miniskirt that Velcro-ed the entire length of the front and a ruffled tank top. When I saw that Jared didn't have a date I was determined to make my move. At the intersection of my seventh daiquiri and third Sam Adams, I summoned enough courage to saunter up beside him. I was never really fond of the taste of alcohol, except for the dessert-y type drinks like daiquiris and pina coladas and a few Sierra Nevada beers that someone else bought for me because they were way too expensive. But taste really didn't matter; alcohol was the Epi-pen to my allergy of trying to connect with people.

The sun was beginning to threaten dawn as I woke up to find Jared rushing around to get dressed, looking for his clothes. He didn't even glance my way as he muttered, "We should just pretend this never happened". Although my recollection of the hours that had passed, between when I sauntered up to him and now, were mere moments: the turn of my top sheet as Jared rolled over, the glimpse of his broad back glistening with perspiration; I could easily fill in the blanks. "You're on the pill, right?" Jared said without turning around. The red of rage began to flush on my cheeks.

I couldn't see it at the time, but I began emulating the ways my dad treated my mom when she didn't behave according to his unspoken expectations. He used manipulation to try to get the love he wanted. Over the next several weeks, Jared continued to ignore me at the diner. I cornered him about 7 a.m. one Saturday morning, while I was juggling a stack of pancakes, over easy eggs and a side of bacon. I reached right in front of him for a bottle of maple syrup on the stainless-steel shelf and looked him square in the eyes. "We need to talk," I said with the tone of voice a High School Principal would use on a student about to get suspended. Color disappeared from his face, "Okay. Okay. Today. When the breakfast rush slows down."

Five hours later, he motioned for me to meet him around back.

In the alley.

I closed the back door and began speaking before I lost my nerve.

"I'm pregnant."

"What?!" he looked quickly to the left then the right.

Checking for witnesses or something.

"Jesus." He started running his hands through his hair so rapidly I thought he'd create bald patches like his brother Jenkins.

"I thought you said you were on the pill?" His voice sounded accusatory.

I had no idea what I said that night.

"I guess it failed." I replied, more meekish than I would've liked.

"I was raised Catholic..." Jared said, with a glazed stare, as if he was talking to his conscience rather than to me. "But you can't keep it. You're not suggesting you want to keep it, are you?" His baritone voice raised a few octaves.

"No. God no. It was one night. I'm not ready to be a mom." Even though I fabricated the whole thing, I could feel tears in my eyes.

"Okay. Okay. Good." Jared slowed the pace of stroking his hair, "I'll give you money for an abortion, then."

I'd replay in my mind, over a million times, the way he said that single sentence.

I don't know what it was about "then" and why, out of the context of the whole situation, that's what stuck. I took his money, knowing I'd use it to buy a gold chain I'd been eyeing at the boutique around the corner. I wore that necklace until I could no longer bear the weight of knowing I'd essentially stolen it.

The thing about blackouts is that, at some point, you have to wake up. My eyes were still closed, glued shut as if they were encased in molasses. I blinked them open at a snail's pace. Then, slightly faster, I blinked them twice. I was suddenly, immediately, terrifyingly awake. I gasped for air. A massive belly was crushing me, imploding my lungs. Above me I recognized the face of Jared's brother, Jenkins. Somewhere in a distant part of my mind I wondered how a man with such a hairy body could have so little hair on his head. Jenkins must have mistaken my gasping for air for excitement as he grunted something garbled that sounded like, "yeah baby." With one final heave, he rolled off of me. Not pausing, I pushed myself off the bed, fumbled for my clothes, and pulled them on as I made my way out the door.

I knew I shouldn't drink like I did. But alcohol served to temporarily chase away my insecurities and my self-hatred. Of course, loathing and doubt would return ten-fold along with the realization of what I'd done the night or nights before. A few weeks after my 'encounter' with Jenkins, I had yet another. I'd only been on a couple of dates with this guy, Jacob, who was known to all of his friends as "Booger." I never asked why.

Wearing the same blue three quarter length strapless dress I'd worn to high school prom, I accompanied Booger to a reunion ball for his college fraternity. The last thing I recall of that evening was getting into Jacob's silver colored 1986 Toyota Celica.

After missing my period the following month, I realized I must've gotten pregnant during a black out the night of Jacob's fraternity reunion ball.

As I contemplated my choices, it made me remember something about my mom. She told me once that she wasn't supposed to have me. The doctors were concerned that after three children, the blood clots that plagued her body would pose a potentially fatal risk in a fourth childbirth. Even my dad told her not to have me. But she insisted on bringing me into the world. When my mom told me, I really wished she hadn't. "You know your father told me I shouldn't have you; the doctors told me I shouldn't have you. I suppose he was just listening to their advice, my blood clots were too severe. How strange that he was worried about losing me..." Her voice trailed off. All this time I thought, *my dad never wanted me.*

Or maybe he just didn't want to lose her: his wife, his love, the mother of his children.

CHAPTER 12

After having an abortion the darkness deep inside threatened to consume me; it became a fierce battle to merely exist. I was twenty two years old and living in a constant state of anxiety. I couldn't open my mail or answer the phone for fear of creditors demanding the money I didn't have. I called my dad once a week out of obligation, I was still financially dependent on him, and in order to pay my rent, I felt like had to kiss his ass.

I was coming to realize that life itself is a choice. I don't think those choices come easy. The choice I made was to terminate the pregnancy. Another woman's choice might not have been my own. At a different moment in my life I might have chosen differently. But every woman has to choose for herself, like my mom did, and like I did.

One Saturday in March, I was sitting on the cold stone ledge of the porch apartment I shared with my roommate. He and I shared an apartment and the same workplace, but rarely saw one another. Just how I like it. I was appreciating a rare Saturday off of work, and just about to enjoy a cigarette and a cup of coffee on the porch, when the phone rang. It was my dad.

"Have you taken the LSAT yet?" It the same question he'd been bombarding me with in every conversation we'd had for the last year. "I thought you were going to register to take it, you're going to Have to take the LSAT if you want any future at all. Don't tell me you're still working at that camping store? You know that no one is going pay you to camp for a living, right? And I didn't work hard all my life and send you to good schools just to have you waste it all…"

His diatribe always went on and on.

Occasionally I would try to break in and say "Dad! I'm just trying to figure out how I can...." But he always cut me off, with the same rant, going on and on about how he didn't raise me just so I could waste my life.

I took a deep drag off the Camel Light and held the black cordless phone away from my head; in part so Alex wouldn't smell smoke on it, but mostly to put distance between my father's voice and my ear.

The last time he called, I put the phone down on the bench near the front door and walked fifty feet away into the kitchen. I washed a sink full of dishes before coming back and picking up the phone again. Like that damn energizer bunny commercial, he was still going. I could have hauled my 90L duffle bag full of dirty clothes to the laundry mat four blocks away, washed, dried and folded three loads of laundry, walked back, and he would have still been talking.

The only thing that ever changed was his volume, the less I agreed with him, the louder he got. It was always a one-person conversation and I couldn't believe I was supposed to take such crap about "wasting my life" from a man who just got out of prison for murder. But he always sent me money for rent, in exchange for the promise that I would find a different job, apply to law school, whatever. It was almost impossible for me to talk to him without having at least a few drinks before, after, and sometimes during our phone call. One hour 'conversation'= one six pack of Pabst (or Sierra Nevada Pale Ale if I could splurge).

It was the summer of 1994, and my father was renting a run down apartment in Peoria Illinois. He said he was doing 'consulting work', which I would later discover was illegal, given that his medical license had been revoked for committing a felony. He had taken a letter he'd received from Alfred University (his alma mater) and illegally created his own letterhead by brazenly typing "Joshua Fierer - Medical & Legal Consultant" right underneath their emblem. And although I didn't know it at the time, he was supplementing his income by dipping into my (and perhaps my siblings) unknown accounts.

Aside from the times I had to deal with him on the phone, I didn't think too much about my dad. I kept trying to moderate my drinking, making pacts with myself that I wouldn't drink this time, or I'd *only have one*. But, just like my parents had, I learned to use alcohol to anesthetize my own painful reality. So I could never keep those promises to myself and always ended up deciding I would just "stop by" the Wrightwood Tap, or the other bar down the street knowing that Tom, a short, awkward guy who had just bought a Harley Davidson Sportster would be there. I had zero attraction to him but I knew he would buy me beers and that I'd probably end up going home with him.

I kept perpetuating a cycle of self-berating and shame; my only momentary relief was that first sip when the bartender put a cold beer into my hand and I chugged the amber colored courage. I drank because I loved the effect it produced; similar to that of gulping air when popping up to the water's surface after a deep free dive. Simultaneously decadent and necessary for survival.

Eventually even that relief was tainted by the impending doom that always followed. I had frequent blackout episodes, and the moment just prior to losing consciousness (most of the time I remained awake- almost like sleepwalking) made me feel like Alice plummeting down the rabbit hole, except instead of the terror she must've felt, I felt total surrender. That is, until I'd come to, and wonder what I had said and done. Then the terror ransacked me like a starving grizzly awoken from hibernation. When I passed out I could feel the details of my depressing life dissolve. In that state I had no responsibility, now awareness, and no memory.

I knew I needed help.

There were other moments that should have been wake up moments, I'd had plenty of them. The old saying goes that sometimes you gotta break down to break through. In yoga class, this is the moment when the teacher has us tighten up all our muscles, or curl into a tight little ball- just before letting it all go for Corpse Pose. The instruction for Corpse pose is supposed to be simple: relax and just lay there. Might be the most difficult thing to do.

My sister Robin had joined a type of therapy group and invited me, in a loving, and slightly codependent way, to join her on a weekend camping retreat with them. She said that she'd pay my way, and promised I didn't have to participate in any of the groups. I was suspicious but I agreed.

The retreat was held in a large cabin in the woods with white interior, hardwood floors and a multitude of cushions on which we all sat. Unknown to me at the time, it was the first of many to come that I'd sit on the floor in a large, openhearted circle.

It was late summer, some of my favorite weather, with warm days and crisp nights. The few times I was outside, the air was filled with the smell of pine needles, the scent of summer's last wildflowers, and cow dung. It was an olfactory premonition of growth and transformation.

Despite my initial resistance, I decided to sit in on one of the first groups of the weekend. It was an opportunity to check everyone out and assess what I, or rather, Robin, had gotten me into. There were about twelve of us there, mostly women, all of whom were older than me. We sat in an amoeba shaped circle, lining the walls of the rectangular-ish shaped room. I listened intently as the others spoke first, talking about big life experiences, and what they meant. When it was my turn, I took a deep breath and said that I was grateful to be there and then, unexpectedly, I told them that I saw it as an opportunity to talk about what I'd never talked about before, namely the death of my mom. It was Robin who admitted to them that our mom had been killed by our father. I didn't know I had stopped breathing, bracing for gasps but the group just held it. I exhaled.

The facilitator, a woman of about fifty, wearing a patchwork long skirt and soft purple tunic top, was gentle and she very carefully encouraged a dialogue between me and Robin. "What does it feel like to be here with your sister talking about such a significant loss?" she asked. Robin admitted that it had been hard to live with it and keep it all in, like pretending that an ulcer didn't exist, ignoring the constant pain and ache. It was the first time that Robin and I had really talked about our mom's murder and how it had affected us. It was a powerful experience of breaking apart the thick silence that had surrounded us since we were children, particularly in the presence of others who seemed to create a safe and sacred space for this unearthing.

Following the retreat, much to my surprise, I continued to meet with a group, but Robin didn't seem so gung-ho about it. She had been seeing a therapist one on one, which worked for her. A woman named Sally, who, with her sagging jowls and beige hair reminded me of a wilting flower, was the first in the group to suggest that most of my problems seemed to stem from my drinking. "Do you think you'd wake up in strange places with strangers if you weren't drinking?" I was shocked at the dichotomy between her appearance and the searing the truth of her question. Sitting on the carpet, I silently drew my knees in towards my chest and wrapped my arms around my shins. Allison, the group facilitator had offered an arrangement when I met with her to tell her I couldn't afford to continue the group. I'd been coming every Wednesday evening for three months, and although I felt it helping on some level, there weren't enough overtime shifts available to cover the $40 a month. "If you'd like to keep coming, I'd love to have you continue. Would you consider doing an exchange? You could help me clean the group space by vacuuming twice a month." Allison's voice covered me with a calm that reminded me of the blanket my mom would heat in the dryer to wrap me in on winter mornings.

"Yes, yes, that'd be good. Thank you."

I used the therapy to find a drinking buddy. We'd throw back a few while gossiping about everyone in the group. Meanwhile the hole at the bottom of my soul continued to spread like moss growing on a tree, preventing light from reaching the bark. Eventually I became desperate enough to listen to the group's suggestions.

At the same time, I also had a sort of love/hate thing going on with food, specifically sugar and carbohydrate-laden foods, like baked goods, ice cream and candy. They continued to be my biggest source of comfort. I binged on these foods and then became disgusted with myself. I would eat things and then put the remainder in the garbage, then in a hungry haste, grab the bag back out of the garbage. I had became a dumpster diver in my own kitchen. Every time I thought I could outsmart myself, and every time I discovered, through deep despair, that I could not control this behavior. I felt even more depressed at the absurdity of it all, and more overweight. At the height of this, I tried running the weight off but it was too hard. And while I often envied those who could make themselves puke, I was never any good at it. I was a weight watchers failure and knew it was bad when I had taken to envying bulimics.

I became willing to go seek help specifically for my eating issues, so I joined another group. It was a droopy sort of group but I heeded their advice, got a mentor who had more experience with these issues than I did, and began to create a food plan. The food plan was a spreadsheet with various categories: protein, grains, fruits, vegetables, etc. Even though I was an educated gal, for some reason it made perfect sense to me, that if I happened to miss some 'grains' in my diet that drinking a beer (or four) could substitute. I actually tried to pass off Hard Cider as a fruit.

When I proudly presented my filled-out-food-plan chart, my mentor read it, looked at me, looked back at the food plan, looked back at me, then put it down, stared me straight in the face and said, "I think you might have a problem with alcohol."

I was aghast and appalled.

Clearly, I thought, I just needed a new mentor.

I didn't think I needed to quit. I had convinced myself that I just needed to learn how to drink more responsibly. But yet another failed attempt at moderating my drinking and waking up with a man I didn't know, made my stomach turn. I couldn't imagine continuing on as I had been, and I couldn't imagine anything different. But I knew that I was probably on the verge of a nervous breakdown, and I finally knew that my sordid affair with alcohol was Over. I could admit that alcohol controlled me, and I recognized that my life was completely out of control, even if I still had no idea what to do about it.

I didn't mind the somewhat cultish crowd at what would turn out to be Jerry Garcia's last show with the Grateful Dead at Soldier Field July 9, 1995. I had every intention of staying with the people I went with. They were from the droopy group abstaining from overeating; but I'd convinced myself that they could be more fun in a different setting, and that they'd be a good influence on me. We'd just found our seats when I caught a whiff of pot and decided to join some people smoking in the row behind us. That was the last thing I remember.

But I was afraid that hanging out with other sober people would feel like being in a cult. So I procrastinated until the Friday before Labor Day weekend of 1995. I pulled down the bill of my dirty, black baseball hat with the US Rowing embroidery on it, beneath it, my eyes darting all around, trying to get a read on everyone. I chose a seat against the back wall right next to the door so if anything too weird started going on, I could bolt. There was a man and a woman sitting up front behind a long card table. The guy was reading off of a laminated piece of paper in a monotone voice. He looked up from the plastic paper as he asked,

"Are there any new people here?"

I looked up to see my hand slowing raising beside my head.

Oh my God, I thought. *That's my hand!*

The guy's voice came alive as he said, "Yes! You in the back, what's your name?"

I quickly debated dashing out the door and never coming back.

"Lisa." I said in the voice of a mouse. I was shocked I didn't say "Alex", the alias I used when out drinking. It'd be years before I discovered that my father was also fond of the use of an alias, or two.

"Welcome!" The room erupted in clapping. And I wondered

what I had done that was so great, "We're glad you're here." The applause subsided, but I was left wondering why any of those people would care if I was there or not. There was a rush of women who surrounded me afterwards, which kinda freaked me out. At that point, I really didn't have any girlfriends and I could not possibly imagine what they wanted from me. I later discovered that they only wanted to share what had so freely been given to them - a life of sobriety. One woman, Jen, nominated herself to guide me through the work of uncovering and discovering what was beneath the surface of my addiction to alcohol.

"You'll need someone to show you the ropes, why don't we go for coffee?" This was more of a demand than a question. Even so, I knew I didn't have money for coffee. "That's okay, I don't really like coffee." I lied. "No problem. You can have tea or water, whatever you like." I knew I wasn't getting out of this. It was the first of many coffee meetings I'd have with Jen, whose personality was much like my father's. Our "conversations" were mostly one sided, with her telling me intricate details of her experience both before she'd quit drinking, and after. Some of her mannerisms even resembled my father's, like those rare moments when she wasn't talking, she'd rest her elbows on the table, her palms pressed together, thumbs holding up her chin, and index fingers pushing up the end of her nose. Although the familiarity would occasionally send shivers down my spine, I'd be forever grateful for her aid. She helped to shed light on the fact that alcohol was but a symptom of what truly ailed me.

In the beginning it was simple: don't pick up a drink, and stay close to other sober people. Admittedly, the not drinking wasn't exactly easy. What was simple was the routine. I hadn't had any kind of daily routine in the ten years between age twelve to twenty two. In boarding school I had spent my waking hours lying to everyone, including myself, cheating on tests, and mass consumption: alcohol, and food, especially cookie dough. The price for all of that showed up in my twenties in the form of as an overly taxed Adrenal/ Immune system. Meaning anytime someone so much as thought of sneezing, I'd get a severe cold or bronchitis.

I didn't tell anyone at work that I'd stopped drinking. And I didn't think that not drinking meant being celibate. So I balked when a friend who was sober actually said, "You don't have anything to offer anyone until you've been clean for a year and begun to clean up the harm to the people you've hurt." I could feel my hands curling into fists at the idea that I couldn't sleep with anyone, (which had been my default way of getting the attention I so deeply craved) until I did all that damn work. Of course I tried to take a shortcut, bargaining in my mind that there couldn't be much harm in doing the work and handing out my phone number to a hot guy.

So when Joe, a handsome dark haired guy appeared in front of me after a meeting one Saturday night, I put my theory to the test. Although I hadn't seen him at that meeting before, I immediately felt at ease with him and we left to get something to eat.

A couple nights later, I'd taken the train to his apartment; a small, dark place with one wall adjacent to the El train. Joe invited me in, but kept the lights so dim I could only make out the outline of the sparse furniture. When the doorbell rang just before dawn, I got a funny feeling in my stomach. He told me it must be the FedEx guy leaving him a package. I was gullible, but not ignorant; I knew by the incessant ringing and Joe's anxiousness, it must be a girlfriend. I began to understand the warnings, and the notion that not everyone came to meetings to change their lives.

Without a drink, I suddenly had no idea what to do with my hands. Especially when I was at a party. I had grown accustomed to holding a drink in one hand and a cigarette in the other. So it felt like my hands had been suddenly fired from their job, after a decade of hard work. It would be years before I learned how to make the outside of my body match the inside of my heart, and how to live peacefully inside my own self.

Often I was appalled at the things sober people said out loud. Everyday I heard people tell stories of stealing from their boss, cheating on their spouse, and abandoning their children. But as horrifying as it was to hear their stories, it was also somewhat intriguing. I'd never heard people declare and own their truth in a way that seemed to be so immensely freeing. Many seemed to have gotten to the proverbial "other side" of whatever painful or humiliating experience they had endured, and were embracing any humor possible. They had found a way to get from hell to hilarious. I wanted that freedom and hoped it was contagious; like any good addict, I just wanted to roll them up and smoke them. I wanted to inhale and absorb their transcendence. But with others I just wanted to smack some happiness Into them, or at the least smack the unhappiness Out of them. Best to begin with myself.

It took me awhile to figure out the distinguishing factor between the people who annoyed me and the ones who intrigued me. What I began to notice was that those who genuinely were the most happy and free were always focusing on the solution rather than the problem; and they were willing to do whatever it took to get into action and be of service to others. They took to the task of shining the light on the dark corners within themselves, uncovering and discovering what fears and beliefs were driving their behaviors. And rather than wasting time wallowing in remorse, they ceased complaining, and did something for someone else. Like calling someone who may be having a difficult time. Offering a ride or, as I've coined: a drive-by hug. The power of a simple act of unexpected kindness is immeasurable.

At one point I told my mentor about climbing into my ex-boyfriend Paul's window, trying to give myself a black eye and bashing in Sandy's car with a 2x4 and she said "Lisa, there are other ways of dealing with hurt and abandonment other than resorting to violence." And in that moment I got it.

My anger had been so much like my dad's anger. And like my dad I was broken, full of hurt and rage, and without any tools to deal with those overwhelming feelings. In the moments of my own violence I had been unable to distinguish what was true from what was false. But I would spend decades wondering if my dad had been able to make that distinction. Attacking a car is not the same as murder, and nothing I said or did or learned could ever bring my mom back to me. I was deeply and fundamentally pissed. I had to begin to create my own sense of right and wrong. These concepts weren't really embodied by my parents, and certainly were not taught to me nor my siblings in a way that we could believe and emulate. So I had to kind of make it up as I went along, particularly in the realm of relationships. As I began to recover, I saw, very clearly, that without right and wrong, good and bad, there is death.

CHAPTER 13

It only took three phone calls, one secret trust fund, one lawsuit, two deaths, eleven million dollars and one gigantic moose to make me finally stand up to my father.

I stepped outside into the freezing air of Anchorage, Alaska, watching the clouds of my breath gathering in front of my face. It was February, 1996. Bundled up in winter gear, I intentionally did not look at the temperature before heading out, knowing that seeing the numbers, especially in single or negative digits, would discourage me from going for a run. The hairs inside my nose formed tiny icicles, but the snowy tree-lined trail was in a valley surrounded by expansive cliffs dotted with iced waterfalls. It was too stunning to pass up, even at –2 degrees.

The path was narrow and the ground textured with drifts of snow. Trees towered over me, covered with thick snow and the only other houses nearby were far more than a stone's throw apart. I always dreamed of moving out west, someplace with more room, more space, more chances to live and play outdoors in nature, instead of being stuck in the concrete jungle of Chicago. Mostly I dreamed of being as far from Morton, Illinois as humanly possible. I wanted to be different and I was ready for my life to be different. Unfortunately, the only things I knew about being in the outdoors were learned from a few summers at Girl Scout camp.

I stepped out onto the path, running slowly, my feet finding their rhythm in the freezing air. After about twenty minutes I came around a bend and ran straight into four thick trees. Shocked, I followed them upward, realizing they weren't trees at all, but massive thick legs. Towering high above me was a full-grown Moose, one of the biggest creatures I had ever seen. His gigantic head was clouded by huge white puffs of breath coming out of his long snout. The rack of his antlers was as enormous as a White House chandelier. Standing, solid and square, he blocked the path. I froze, trying to remember which animals to run from, which ones to run towards and which ones to supposedly stand my ground. In fact, that moment was a perfect metaphor for my lifelong struggle to understand how to handle the men in my life: my boyfriends, my bosses, my father.

I stood perfectly still, not breathing, waiting. Then the most extraordinary thing happened, as I stood my ground, the moose slowly backed away, his massive dark shape disappearing into the woods. Although calm in that moment, after he was gone, a wave of terror hit me. Realizing how close I had just come to dying, I raced back to the house where I was staying, still shaking, still in awe.

Less than three hours later, the phone rang.

My lawyer, Robert Chapman, was calling. "Call me Bob," he'd said when I first met him. I'd quickly learn he was a man who wore his heart on his sleeve; a fact which made me continually forget that he was a lawyer.

"Lisa?" I could hear Chapman's voice soften through the phone.

"Yeah?" my voice was shaking. It was years before cell phones and I'd only left this number at my friend Aaron's house in case of emergency. I gripped the wooden side of the futon to brace myself.

"Lisa, not only did we clarify that there is indeed a Trust in your name, called Trust Fund #4 with approximately $250,000 in it, we also found the specific withdrawals that your father has made from that account. You've got a very solid case here but I wanted to talk things over with you; I know you're out of town, but I believe your father and his lawyers will act quickly." My mind was reeling. *Are you kidding me? $250,000? Wasn't that a quarter of a million dollars? Could my father really be doing this? Wouldn't he have needed my signature on something? How could he get away with it?*

I don't think either Chapman or I ever said the word "lawsuit" out loud. It was always referred to as, "pursuing legal action" which had a much more casual feel to it, like buying a lottery ticket. All I wanted was for my father to be held accountable for his behavior; behavior that had the IRS coming after me. Since my dad continually refused to answer (or even acknowledge) my direct questions over the past six months about why the IRS was sending me notices, I thought maybe he'd listen to the Courts. But one way or the other it was now official: my father had been committing fraud in my name and I was officially suing him.

It started nine months earlier, when the taste of metal clung to my teeth as I opened the first mysterious letter from the Internal Revenue Service. I wished my roommate Asher wasn't home. Asher and I worked together at an outdoor retail store on Armitage St. in Chicago. It was a matter of convenience that we were roommates and the situation seemed to work well for both of us. Asher spent more time hanging out on the sofa with Harley, my Siberian Husky puppy, than me.

I came home from work that night about 7:30 p.m. and from the front door, I heard an unearthly howling,

"oooowwwwwwweeeuuuuuuuu"

I jostled my key in the lock, flung open the door and saw Asher, his shoulder length, brown curly hair sticking straight out from his small head. What Asher lacked in height, he made up tenfold in personality. His mouth was wide open as he howled with Harley, who was sitting on the couch beside him, his fur all tousled, like he and Asher had been wrestling. My entrance didn't deter either one of them. I looked at the TV, the sound silenced beneath their howling. The cartoon Tom and Jerry was on; I wondered if their shenanigans were the result of something Tom or Jerry did or if they were just howling for the hell of it.

Although Asher and I shared living space, work-space and time with my dog, there was much I didn't share with him. I didn't tell him that I often smoked cigarettes in the alley behind our apartment, or that I had recently quit drinking and was trying desperately to stay sober, or that my father had been out of prison for four years since his felony conviction.

One of the only things I enjoyed about my life was that I kept it compartmentalized. It seemed easier to just pick up the mail, walk past their playing and go straight to my room to open the terrifying government envelopes. Typically I avoided the mail, but my friend Mo kept encouraging me to open it and to start actually answering my phone – she said this is what 'normal' people do. "Lisa," she said "Now you're equipped to handle life on life's terms. Not drinking means facing what's happening, no matter what. You gotta begin to trust that you can handle it."

Thankfully, I no longer received handwritten letters from my father with his prison return address: Joshua Fierer, Southern Illinois Correctional Facility and his Inmate Number stamped neatly in the corner. But I had only been opening the mail for a month and even tearing open junk mail made me queasy. I was trying to live my new non-drinking life with honesty, integrity and responsibility, but the five brown IRS envelopes I held in my hand made me think that maybe I should have started opening the mail a bit sooner. I sat on my bed, swallowed my fear, and opened the most recent one.

"*Dear Ms. Fierer,*

We are writing to collect a debt. Any and all communications are being documented in the effort to collect the following amount in arrears:

$15,690.82

You are responsible for paying this amount for the following reason(s):

Funds were withdrawn from accounts listed in your name without proper taxation paid for the duration of the following time periods:

1990, 1991, 1992, 1993, 1994

The amount reflected above does not include additional costs incurred in the attempts to retrieve proper payment of this debt. You are responsible for all such costs, including but not limited to..."

At that point, I stopped reading. *How the heck could I possibly owe them thousands of dollars?* I was in my last year of college, racking up more in student loans than credit hours, working two jobs at minimum wage and still dependent on my dad to help pay the rent in my rodent infested apartment. I was under the impression that I did my part regarding taxes every year by dutifully sending off my W-9's and related paperwork to our longtime family accountant Mr. Hannaway. As long as I always sent him all my tax stuff by April 1st, I figured I was fine. I didn't receive anything back from Mr. Hannaway prior to his filing my taxes and I didn't know that in order to legally file them, my signature had to be on the final form submitted. I was 22 and apparently should have been signing my own tax returns for the past 4 years; I didn't know any better.

Opening the other four letters from the IRS, all said the same thing: I owed them money, a lot of money. But I still had no idea why. I called my dad to ask him about it but he was evasive and feigned ignorance. A week later I received another letter from the IRS and things went from bad to worse.

> *"Dear Ms. Fierer,*
> *There has been no response regarding the information*
> *requested on the filing of your tax return for the years 1990,*
> *1991, 1992, 1993, and 1994. Therefore, you have incurred an*
> *additional penalty of $3,922.70 for a total due $19,613.52.*
> *The next course of action is a levy. Contact a representative*
> *with questions regarding your account, to set up a payment*
> *plan or send payment in the amount of: $19,613.52 to*
> *Department of the Treasury , Internal Revenue Service*
> *Center, Kansas City, MO 64999-0099"*

The next course of action is a levy. A levy?

All I could think of was Don McLean singing, "drove my Chevy to the levy but the levy was dry...." *Wait, was that "levy" or "levee"?* After some phonetic procrastination, I called my friend Mo. We agreed I would call my dad yet again and try to find out exactly what was going on. And, if he didn't give me any answers, I was prepared to call the IRS myself. She helped me fill out small index cards with things to say to my dad in case I got intimidated or overwhelmed, just like the ones I had used on the debate team in school. Despite the fact that I was finding it nearly impossible to have a phone conversation with my dad and stay sober, I took a leap of faith and called him.

"Dad?" The cards trembled in my shaking hands.

"Fleabop! how are you?"

My teeth clenched as I heard him use this nickname he imposed on me—I never found it endearing.

"I'm ok. But I'm concerned about this letter I just received. It's another one from the IRS again and it says I owe a *lot* of money."

"Oh just send it to me, I'll take care of it."

"Dad, you've said this before and clearly something is not being taken care of. Why can't I just run this by you over the phone and maybe you can help me decipher it." It came out more like a statement than a request, probably because I was reading off the note cards. I could hear his voice tighten. And that scared me.

"I Said I'll take care of it."

But I wasn't bending, not this time. My voice shook as I said, "Dad. This is serious. It's a huge debt, in my name, and I need to get to the bottom of it."

There was a pause and I pulled out my final note card. "So I'll be calling the IRS after you and I get off the phone." I could hear him snort in disgust.

"Oh, I'm sure you'll enjoy being on hold for at least an hour."

The conversation ended shortly after that, it was the same cyclical conversation that we always had. My dad was a master at answering just enough to keep me engaged and hopeful but I always knew it was never the whole truth.

It was time to call the IRS, ask them for some clarity about the amount owed, tell them that I was trying to get to the bottom of this, and would be fully accountable. First I called Mo. I was beginning to learn this skill referred to as, 'bookending': the practice of calling for support before a difficult discussion or event and calling afterwards. Mo and I said a little prayer. "You can do this, Lisa! Know that you are well supported and that someday, your experience of getting through something tough, with grace, will inspire someone else to do the same."

With trembling fingers, I dialed (800) 829-1040. Thankfully there was no wait time, I'm sure I would have chickened out.

"Internal Revenue Service, can I help you?" I heard a faint southern twang in the woman's voice.

"Um, yeah, I um, am calling aboutthischargethatyousayiowebutidontunderstandatall" I should have breathed between words. "Sure, let me pull up your account and we'll figure it all out." She had a warm way about her, dispelling all my beliefs and fears about making this call. Ms. Sanders looked up my account and sure enough, I owed $15,690.82 plus charges in unpaid taxes. That was more money than I'd earned in my life thus far. She was incredibly kind, removed some of the charges and helped me set up a small monthly payment to buy me some time to figure out what the hell was going on.

While talking about the IRS problem in my therapy group, Allison, the group facilitator, suggested that I speak with her dear friend Georgeanna who was a financial advisor. Desperate for some help, I called her. "Oh, my goodness, let's figure this out!" she exclaimed. Her voice sounded as inviting as warm homemade banana bread. Shortly thereafter, we met in person; she listened to my ramblings about my dad, the IRS, etc. and she became one of the very few I had talked to about losing my mom and all of the craziness with my dad.

She suggested, after reading the IRS letters, that there was probably an account (or multiple accounts) in my name that perhaps I didn't know about, on which taxes weren't being paid and since I had already reached 18, I was responsible for paying those taxes. Georgeanna also suggested that, since my dad wasn't relinquishing any information, I might want to "seek legal counsel".

Georgeanna gave me the names of three attorneys she recommended and proposed that I call each one and 'interview' them. I really didn't want to go into all the gory details about my dad murdering my mom. Calling the first guy on the list, I summarized my life and situation in two minutes, after which there was a slight pause. I stopped chewing on my fingernails when Mr. Chapman began to share that he knew exactly who my father was. A number of years ago, he provided legal representation to his own father against my dad in a lawsuit that my dad had initiated. Too consumed by the sheer coincidence to ask for any details about that lawsuit, I thought, "if it's Odd, it's God." Chapman already knew all the nuances of dealing with my father. He agreed that the IRS thing sounded suspicious and agreed to look into it.

That February, I was invited to go ice climbing with two guys from work. I was surprised to be invited, but it sounded like fun and I had always wanted to see Alaska. The three of us camping store coworkers stayed in a friend's house, a classic A-frame cottage. Typically I often wing it when I travel, as opposed to the meticulous way my father memorized the layout of a place to which he travelled. Reading a bit on Alaska, I was delighted to learn that it is over twice the size of Texas, home to millions of lakes and is the only state whose capital city is accessible solely by air or ship, since there are no roads that connect Juneau to the rest of the continent. It made me want to move West.

In addition to ice climbing, I badly wanted to see the pre-race for the famed Iditarod dog sled race. I had been dog sledding before, but this was different. Everywhere there were large customized trucks carrying sled dogs. Each truck had dozens of tiny cages with little steel doors, stacked on top of one another.

For a moment, it reminded me of my three siblings. Sue was in Colorado raising my niece Brooke-Lynn and nephew Darrell; Robin lived in Chicago but we were no longer roommates and didn't see each other very often. Jonny was living in Minnesota and no doubt had a host of friends; he could get a three-toed sloth to cut a rug on the dance floor.

Each of us were living in separate spaces, separate corners, divided by the little steel doors of everything that had happened in our lives as a family. Little did I know that soon I would be asking them to pull with me to haul our father to Court.

After my encounter with the massive Moose and Chapman's phone call telling me about Trust Fund #4, I was pretty fired up. Returning to Chicago, I called my brother and sisters. "If this is Trust #4, then you can bet that there are three others, one in each of your names, "I said. "These are accounts no one ever told us about; accounts we are responsible for. Dad's been using our names and identities, without our permission, hasn't paid taxes on money he's taken out of mine and probably yours as well! Don't you want to join me in this lawsuit to get back what is rightfully ours?" While they agreed that nothing involving our father was very straightforward nor simple, they had kids to raise and credit cards to pay off and a thousand other concerns. I suppose they were wary of poking at the hornet's nest that was our dad. In the end, they chose not to join me in the lawsuit but they told me they understood what I was doing and that I had to do it.

During the course of the lawsuit, my grandmother, (my dad's mother, Grandma Poppi) died. I hadn't been in contact with her nor my dad's dad (Poppi) for more than a year. I couldn't. They were still pretending that they had a wonderful son who could do no harm, and I could no longer participate. When Grandma Poppi died, I grappled with whether or not to go to her funeral. One moment I'd think, *I'm not gonna* let seeing my dad, who's being a total dick wad to me, prevent me from paying my respects to her. Then I'd think, "Did I respect her? She always stood by my father, who'd done horrible things, and never stood up against her husband who treated her like a piece of furniture." Fear won the fight I had with myself; I didn't go. The truth was, I was still terrified of my father. Three months later, almost to the day, Poppi passed away. Again, I struggled whether or not to go, and again, I was incapacitated by fear. My emotions felt like a soggy grocery bag, ready to give way and spill its contents all over the sidewalk. I didn't think I could do it, sober. I'd have to honor them in my own way, at another time.

CHAPTER 14

I saw him look at me across the dimly lit church basement. I wasn't there to pray, I was desperately searching for a new community to connect with. I'd just moved to Boulder, Colorado two weeks before and I was sober for a little over a year. The outdoor gear company I worked for decided to open a store in Boulder and I was invited to move there to help run the shop. One of the managers had a friend who had recently rented a townhouse in Boulder and was in need of a roommate, so I landed a place for Harley and me to live without too much drama.

I was thrilled to finally move out West, but knew I needed to find others who also didn't drink. The vast change from drinking to the point of blacking out to breaking up with booze necessitated creating new everyday patterns that were vital to my well-being.

Even from across the room he looked like trouble. 6'3, about 225 lbs, with short dark hair and the kind of hazel eyes that adjusted to whatever color shirt he wore. One side of his mouth was upturned in a sort of mischievous grin. He sauntered over to me and said "Hey, my name's Rich Hardt". I had promised Mo and myself that I wouldn't get involved with anyone until I was settled in my life in Boulder for at least a year. I was so nervous that out of the clear blue sky I blurted, "Look, it'll be a long cold summer before we ever get together!" Instead of running away from the crazy girl, he just laughed, turned up the wattage on his grin and said, "Isn't that a Jimi Hendrix line?" Little did I know that I had just waved a red flag in front of a bull.

Rich was working on sobriety too, although I'd learn that

what he called working on sobriety looked more like picking up women who were working on sobriety. But a week later, he brought me a hoagie on my lunch break at the shop. The store was on the west end of Pearl Street, a brick-lined outdoor mall in downtown Boulder. Pearl Street was like Mayberry with its fountains and beautiful flowerbeds, only it wasn't fiction. The Boulder Flatirons, flat angular slabs of granite, marked the edge of the Rocky Mountain range, towering over the western edge of town.

"This," Rich said handing over the paper wrapped foot-long sandwich with mock solemnity, "is the best sandwich in the world." I rolled my eyes. But the truth was, I appreciated his attention. Rich seemed nice. He noticed details that other people often overlooked, like the look in the panhandler's eyes that silently said he missed his daughter and tiny carvings etched into the base of a wooden bridge I'd walked over a hundred times and hadn't seen. He had a wicked sense of humor, delightfully dry that never failed to make me laugh.

After those first few weeks we began seeing each other a lot, both of us lying belly-down on my bed like ten year olds, lost in deep conversations about our families and our pasts. I told him about how my mom died; he listened intently and had a depth of understanding that didn't match his smirk-y exterior. Rich had mastered the art of odd jobs. Whether he was fixing a fence for an older woman whose dog had escaped or running errands for a wealthy couple, he waited for jobs that no one else wanted to fall in his lap. But it seemed that what he really wanted to do was retire by the age of thirty.

His attention and devotion came with something else I should have seen coming: a whole lotta cheating. By the time we'd been dating six months, we had already broken up two or three times.

Every time I got tired of his infidelities and lies I would dump him, but then he would sweet talk his way back. He'd cash his ticket back in the moment I'd second-guess my own intuition. I would tell myself that Rich was not quite the guy I thought he was and to leave his cheating ass, and then I would convince myself, *Maybe that beautiful girl who showed up at his house when we were napping really was just his buddy's ex-girlfriend.* After a while of our push-me-pull-me relationship, his humor grew crueler, his insults more spiked with personal and intimate details I had shared with him when my guard was down. I finally got angry, decided that enough was enough and broke up with him for good.

I drove over to his place late one Sunday morning in March to get back some of the stuff that I had given him: a pair of Carhartt jeans and a couple flannel shirts. I pulled into Rich's driveway and left the tailgate of my Dodge Durango standing open after taking my dog Harley out to come with me.

I went around the back of the house to the basement apartment he shared with his friend Ted. I knocked on the door and Rich answered it. He was wearing boxers and a faded hunter green T-shirt. He let me in and I saw that he had gathered all of my stuff into a messy pile by the door. It looked like a load of laundry that someone had been too high to do so they left it for, like, a year.

"I can't believe you're really taking back all the gifts you gave me," he said, his thick hands curling into fists. "Well," I said, "If I'd known what a dickhead you are, I wouldn't have bought you gifts in the first place."

He leaned back against the wall and methodically crossed his arms in front of his chest. He stood perfectly still and looked at me with a smile that was less a smirk and more of a dagger of ice aimed at my chest.

"You're a fucking bitch," he said, still unmoving, "And an Indian giver."

I knew enough about the history of Native Americans to truly understand the insult and the words hit me hard. In the back of my mind a small bell began to ring, *it sounds like something my father would say.* My father, like Rich, loved American history. Both of them knew the names of famous western battles and generals, but for all of their supposed respect for the native community, neither one would pass up an opportunity for a cruel slur when the chips were down, especially if it made them look clever or to gain the upper hand.

Standing there in the hallway, my arms full of shirts and jeans and shit I didn't really want I said, "Yeah? Well at least I'm not a fucking liar!"

Suddenly there was a blur of motion and animal heat. In an instant, his wide fingers encircled my throat. Gasping for air, I wondered how he'd moved so fast in a split second. His grip tightened around my neck and he lifted me off the ground with one hand, throwing me up against the wall.

I slammed hard, gulping for air. My body slid down the wall, limp and dizzy with dark spots dancing in front of my eyes. I sat on the floor, heart pounding, clutching at my throat. Finally I looked up and he was gone. He had vanished, and for a minute my head spun, I wondered *did that really just happen?*

Just then, his roommate Ted came out of his room. Although Rich complained about him often, Ted was the perfect roommate for him. When Ted saw me on the floor, he just sort of shuffled around me. It wasn't the first time I wondered if Ted had suffered some mild form of brain damage from his excessive drinking.

Finally able to breathe, I stood up, stepped over the bundle of clothes and ran for the door.

Harley had already run silently to the back of my Durango. In some detached part of my mind I noted that my husky, notorious for running away at any opportunity, was guiding me to safety. Jumping behind the wheel, I locked the door and tears hit me like a tsunami. I pushed the shifter into drive and pulled out onto the street, sobbing so hard I didn't even see the bright red stop sign in front of me until I heard the crunch of metal.

I had hit a beige Honda Accord broadside, but thankfully we had both been going slowly through the intersection. An older man got out of the driver's side, looking startled and shaken up. Somehow, I managed to put my Durango in park and turned my head when he tapped lightly on my window.

"Are you ok?" He asked when I rolled my window down, "Are you hurt? What happened?"

"I'm so sorry" I sobbed, "I just had a fight with my boyfriend. He threw me up against a wall, choked me and I hit my head, I..."

The man's face was horrified, "Oh my god are you ok?" he looked down, seeing the red welt on my throat as I fought to catch my breath yet again, then he looked up and down the street. "Don't worry, I'm going to get you some help." Then he ran to the nearest house to call the cops.

After a few minutes, both a male cop and female cop showed up. I was still crying as they took my statement and assessed the damage. Miraculously both vehicles were still drive-able and we both walked away unhurt; the police were more concerned about the attack. Informing me that Colorado has a mandatory arrest law for domestic violence calls, they issued a warrant and placed Rich under arrest. To my surprise, there was already an outstanding warrant on him for a traffic violation and he was taken into custody.

One of the things the police asked me was if I wanted to talk to an advocate from the Boulder County Safehouse, a local non-profit that specialized in offering support, counseling and a safe haven to people who have been the victims of domestic violence. With my mind still reeling from the two collisions, I agreed, and a woman from Safehouse showed up within the hour. She was in her thirties and had a calm, supportive vibe. "I know this is hard," something in her voice made me believe her, "We just try to help walk you through it and provide support if you want." She seemed respectful of my emotional state and asked me if I needed shelter, giving me info about what was available. I told her I felt ok, but in the weeks that followed I found myself thinking about my parents and of their many fights and the restraining orders. I knew how fast violence could happen. As a child, I had been witness to domestic violence almost every day, but now I was on the inside. My anger at feeling so helpless was compounded by my frustration with the legal system.

With the help of another Safehouse advocate, called a Court Advocate, I filed a restraining order against Rich. He then countered by filing one against me, which I learned was typical. I was pissed at how easy it was for him to file one against me, and noticed on the copy that was sent to me that he messed up my birthdate. He had written the date my mom was killed, three days after my birthday.

I decided to forgo pursuing any further legal action against Rich. Then I received correspondence from the court on which Rich's attorney had stated, "Lisa is litigious and any further efforts on her part to pursue legal action against my client should be regarded as such." Of course, I thought, Rich told his attorney about me suing my dad. That should not have surprised me. But it wouldn't be the first or the last time that I expected decent behavior from a man who behaved similarly to my dad.

Despite what Rich may have believed or claimed in his defense, I never really wanted to sue my father. It felt as though my dad left me no choice but to involve the law. Even so, it wasn't an easy ride. I dreaded the calls from my attorney and especially the few conference calls with both my father and my legal counsel. There's no right way to sue your father for stealing your money and your identity. Every call made me feel pigeonholed. All I wanted to do was get the help of the courts in holding my father accountable for the money I owed, money that he took.

At the same time the restraining orders against each of us lapsed, the start of my five-year bout with insomnia began. If I could fall asleep, it was rarely before 4 a.m. For months, I existed on two or three hours of sleep a night, which felt more like exhaustion than rest. As I lay there, trying to will myself to sleep, the coversheet bound around my ankles was the only thing keeping me from tossing and turning. Like when I was a kid and Mom stayed in my bed or we slept in the parking lot of the motel, my nervous system was alert, ready to pounce on any possible threats. Ironically, I had again become my own worst enemy.

I began seeing a counselor at Safehouse, a woman named Sam who was about my age. In our weekly conversations in the upstairs of the house that had been converted into Safehouse's Community Outreach Center, she helped me see that my relationship with Rich demonstrated how deeply the patterns of domestic abuse are embedded, and that those patterns are often intricate and complicated.

Each time I left the Safehouse Outreach Center, I had some version of this thought: *what if I spent more time there; I wonder if there's something I could do...* I finally got up the nerve to ask Sam if there was any way to get involved. I learned I wasn't the only one who'd had such thoughts. So many, in fact, that they had a policy requiring nine months after receiving services from Safehouse before applying for volunteer positions.

I finally made it as a Children's Volunteer. One Wednesday evening, while I was cleaning up glitter from an art activity I was facilitating, I realized that my desire to volunteer was to give a small part to others, a part of safety and support that my mom never got to experience. I wished that she had been offered a safe place to go when my dad flew into one of his rages. If any Safehouse existed in central Illinois in the early 1980's, we never heard about it.

Less than two years later, my job at the outdoor company ended and I moved from being a volunteer at Safehouse to taking a job with them as a Community Educator. Despite my inherent fear of public speaking, I had a strong desire to spread awareness about domestic violence and confront the myths, stereotypes and silence surrounding it. The morning I signed my employment contract with Safehouse was a pivotal moment. Finally I was moving towards something that I had always moved away from. Instead of running from my demons, I signed a contract to face them and help others do the same.

In my years spent working there, I learned more about the dynamics of domestic abuse than I ever wanted to know, including the fact that women are up to 85 % more at risk of being killed by their partner just after leaving the relationship. Intimate partner death is so common against women that there is actually a word for it:

Femicide.

Hearing that statistic for the first time, I felt as if I'd been socked in the stomach by my dad, by Rich, by a million men filled with rage. I remembered the feel of my feet running out the door of Rich's place, not knowing if he was behind me or not. I recalled the solid metal clunk of my car door when it closed; Harley panting and whining in the back seat as I tore out of his driveway. But I also remembered all those years I'd seen my mother hiding a black eye, or the sparkle in her eyes that had been punched out, worn thin and gone. But more than skin, tissue and bone, my dad had punched out hope. I told her again and again, "you gotta leave Dad, you just gotta get out of here." I began saying that before I was seven years old.

As a Community Educator, I had the opportunity to address the perpetual stereotype that aids in Femicide:

'Why doesn't she just leave?'

Although I kept my personal experience quiet, as was required by my job, in order to maintain focus on the women, families and communities with whom we worked, I felt like my learning went alongside the students I was teaching. I shared statistics and information with students in university ethics classes; I also presented at schools of massage therapy so that massage thera-pists and bodyworkers would be equipped to provide resources to a woman experiencing domestic abuse. The two-hour courses always began with an exercise designed to debunk the common myths about domestic violence. I'd set the group up in a circle and begin to ask True/False questions. Those who believed the statement to be 'true' were asked to stand over on the right side of the room; 'false', to the left. The statements were designed to target the essence of the students' belief, for example:

"If a woman is given a black eye by her partner, she should

leave him immediately."

Like me, many of the folks in these classes had some initial resistance to this excavation process. The material touched a few, angered some, and others probably forgot it entirely. But I was determined to plant seeds of opportunity for each student to question their own beliefs, behaviors and judgments around women's safety and well-being. I especially wanted to cultivate an awareness of the way we perpetuate and normalize violence towards women through our own language. White tank top undershirts are frequently called, "wife beaters" and I couldn't even count the times I heard both men and women use the phrase, "bitch slapped".

Although I was gaining knowledge and confidence in my work with Safehouse, my relationship with my dad was far from resolved. I was three years into the slow-moving lawsuit against my father for control of "Trust #4", and just like the first one, the second big lawsuit bombshell happened when I was out for a run. It was July of 1999 and supposed to be a scorcher of a day, so I was out early, headed up the Eldorado Mountain trail in the 7 a.m. cool morning air. The sharp canyon walls always felt like a geological hug at the start of the trailhead. And then, all of a sudden, it would open up into an expansive field. Just as I headed up the trail my cell phone rang. The area code was (312), which I recognized immediately as Chicago. It was 8 o'clock their time, the very start of the working day. Although cell phones had been out for a number of years, this was my very first one and it always surprised me when it rang.

"This is Lisa." I said, attempting to sound relaxed although I'd just been running uphill.

"Lisa, this is Joel Friedman." No wonder I didn't recognize

the entire number; Mr. Friedman never called me directly, it was always Robert Chapman, the friendlier of the two attorneys who worked on the case against my dad. Friedman was an efficient shark-like attorney; Robert Chapman was more of the get-along-with-everyone kind of guy. Together they made a dynamic duo.

"Yes, sir?" I was terrified of Friedman from the first meeting. The last time I'd called someone "Sir" I was talking to the principal in Junior High.

"Lisa," Joel paused, for perhaps the first time ever.

"There's been a shift in the case that we need to address."

I held my breath.

"Your father was made Executor of his father, Norman Fierer's estate. Your grandparents Norman Fierer and his deceased wife Evelyn Fierer have left your father in charge of Eleven Million Dollars." Right there, in the middle of Eldorado Canyon, I nearly pissed myself. *How many zeros is that exactly??*

Joel didn't miss a beat.

"Now, your father has threatened to file a Motion to remove you from your grandfather's Will unless you drop the case you have initiated against him."

My fear of Friedman disappeared and my anger, like the fresh film of sweat on my skin, came pouring out; I practically cut him off.

"I'm sorry, let me get this straight: either I relinquish entitlement to my grandfather's estate or I drop the lawsuit that we've been pursuing for the last three years?"

" Yes," he said, "so think about what you want your next course of action to be."

I hung up the phone, put it in my pocket and began to run again. My legs and lungs bore the brunt of my rage. I was never a very fast runner, until that moment. I wanted to outrun the reality of what was happening. I poured my emotions through my body and my arms, fists clenched, pumping to propel myself higher, faster, to a place beyond my thoughts. The timing of this was terrible; it had just seemed as though there was an end in sight to the lawsuit against my dad. I had decided, nine months earlier that, in order to preserve my sanity, I could have no contact with my father whatsoever. No conference calls, and I had my lawyers read me the parts of letters in correspondence from my dad and his attorney that I needed to know.

I vowed to not let this new twist of events twist me up and with the help of my therapist and close knit crew, went about the business of working through it all. "It's so f-cking unfair!" I'd whine. To which I'd hear, "Yes, many things are unfair. Our job is to find a place of peace so that the things happening around us, fair, unfair, you name it, don't pitch us off course." And that was the start of what became my mantra: 'I'd rather have peace, than get a piece'.

Since I didn't play the lotto, this was my closest encounter with major money. Money I didn't even know existed in my family. Poppi and Grandma Poppi, Norman and Evelyn, were Depression era Jews. Hardworking, Orthodox Jews – not Ultra Orthodox, but they kept kosher and obeyed the Sabbath – sort of. They observed only so far as it would appear to their Orthodox neighbors that they were observing the Sabbath. In other words, they would keep the lights off that were visible to their neighbors, but would use the ones that were out of sight. Observing these unexplained ironies, I believed that religion was really about what others think you are doing or not doing rather than what you believe. It would be a number of judgmental years before I'd hear and begin to practice the spiritual suggestion, "Be quick to see where religious people are right. Make use of what they offer." Even so, it would continue to baffle me that they hadn't bought new underwear for themselves in decades.

I knew this for a fact because my grandmother always hung the laundry on the clothesline alongside their garage. As a child I'd watch her from the kitchen in their Brooklyn three-flat. She had no shame in clothes-pinning Poppi's threadbare tighty-whities and her oversized undies (with the elastic unraveled) to the clothesline for the world to see. They were fairly generous with us and would send money for birthdays and Chanukah, but I always thought of them as proud but working-class poor.

Man, was I ever wrong about that.

CHAPTER 15

Gravel crunched beneath the tires as we pulled into the parking lot of the Stanley Hotel. As my friend Kathy put her car in park I declared, "I'm not getting out."

In her omni-loving way, Kathy turned to me with a smile, took my hand in hers and said,

"Okay. But just be sure that you can live with whatever decision you choose."

I knew she was right, I was both grateful for her spiritual centeredness and pissed off by it at the same time. I sat for a moment, wondering if my shortness of breath had anything to do with the thousand plus feet of altitude we gained in driving from Boulder to Estes Park. Or maybe I was having an anxiety attack. *I don't really know what an anxiety attack is. I thought. God, I do not want to be here. I do not want to do this. Why do I have to do This?* My legs felt like liquid.

"I'm not hugging him...," I said.

"You have a choice here," Kathy said "to totally trust God with this, or you can try and manage it yourself. We'll just show up and you can leave the details to God. If and when we need to, we can go."

Just as she said that, a wave of courage returned to my legs; they felt solid, strong. I opened the passenger door and planted my feet firmly on the ground, then lifted the rest of my body up and out of the car. As I was closing the car door, my back to the Hotel, I could literally feel my dad coming towards me. I cringed, wondering if maybe I could just never turn around. I would rather face the car door indefinitely than face my father.

I turned around.

We were having a Fierer Family Reunion. Well, not quite a reunion, it was more like a gathering. A few weeks earlier, I had gotten a voicemail from my brother Jonny that our dad had wanted to get all of us together and, through my brother, had extended a specific invitation to me. It was the summer of 2003 the world was a few years away from Hurricane Katrina, and I was a few years away from the lawsuit against my father. It was resolved in a winning settlement split six ways to benefit my three siblings, my sister Sue's two kids and me. I had to concede what I really wanted: a full acknowledgement of my father's actions and impacts on me, my brother and sisters. Instead I accepted a full severance of financial ties to my/our father.

Jonny's voicemail began, "It's your brotha. Hey, Dad wants us all to get together. He said, 'be sure to call your sister Lisa to invite her' ".

My dad has always done that - referring to us as "Your sister" or "Your brother." As if we only belonged to one another, a subtle stab at disowning all four of us.

Jonny's message continued, "So I made reservations for us at the Stanley Hotel in Estes, you know, where they filmed *The Shining!* It'll be the perfect place for us to all get together." His voicemail ended with giggling to himself, a reminder that humor (the more warped the better) had served us well in surviving the absurdity and chaos that we simply referred to as: Family.

Due to the fact that talking to my father was a ten-drink minimum for me, I took a seven-year sabbatical from him, which had helped me maintain my sobriety. For whatever reason, I now knew deep down that it was time to see him. I immediately called Kathy and told her about Jonny's message and my sense that, for reasons unknown to me, I needed to be there. Even though it seemed about as much fun as poking my eye out with a sharp stick.

I met Kathy shortly after she moved to Boulder. Although she's a slender woman with a tender smile, Kathy has a 'big mama' kind of presence: loving and embracing, but sharp as a whip and willing to do anything to protect those she cares about. Which is pretty much everyone. She has this uncanny way of immediately putting people at ease. She became a mentor to me and a stand-in mother for the one I spent every day missing.

I shouldn't have been surprised when Kathy offered to go with me to this odd family gathering.

"However, I can be supportive," she said, "you just let me know."

I began to consider her offer, even through my disbelief. Why would someone willingly spend time surrounded by four siblings full of resentment towards their father, and the father who lived in a bubble of denial – a world of his own creation that he imposed on everyone around him?

I started walking across the wide driveway at the Stanley and there he was, walking towards me. Striding, really. As if he had a personal competition with gravity that he was determined to win. As I watched, I began to sense that he too was nervous. "Fleabop!" he called to me, and I cringed.

He put his arms out and I hugged him. It just kinda happened, in an organic hugging sort of way. In doing so, I realized that I was almost taller than him. And that the fabric on his ancient polo shirt was nearly threadbare at the shoulders – probably where it rubbed against the old navy sport coat he often wore for 'dressy occasions'. I noticed his hair was completely white and he looked much smaller than I recalled. This monster of a man was just my aging, shrinking Dad.

I introduced Kathy, a welcome distraction to the flood of emotions washing over me. My dad immediately shifted into his charming, "Oh, it's so nice to meet you" mode. I dissociated from their idle chatter to steal a moment in my own mind and body, to regain my emotional composure so that I could handle what was just ahead, an entire meal with Dad, his mysterious 'lady friend', my three siblings and niece and nephew. Anything could happen.

As Kathy and I followed my dad to the hotel entrance, I realized that Kathy's red hair, like my mothers, had taken on a chilling new meaning as we walked behind my father. I felt the gravity of this thought all the way into my legs which had turned to lead as I tried to lift them up the wide, white concrete steps leading to the hotel entrance. The three of us entered the foreboding foyer of the Stanley. The maroon velvet curtains shoved the sunshine away, despite the enormous windows. The heavy, Victorian style furniture discouraged any possible playfulness. I silently cursed Jonny and tried to remember how funny it seemed to have a family reunion at the 'Shining' hotel.

Even though they chose differently, Jonny, Sue and Robin ultimately supported my decision to not talk to our father. All four of us had, at one time or another, gotten so angry with Dad and his denial, that we didn't talk to him for maybe a week or a month at most. But I was the only one who had taken the last seven years 'off' from having any type of relationship with Dad at all.

Of the four siblings, Sue looked the most like our father: dark hair and hazel eyes. Robin, Jonny and I all had the same coloring: towheaded toddlers, our curly locks and light blue eyes carried into adolescence. Robin had begun a career as a school psychologist and although Dad tried to beat the artistic nature out of our brother Jonny, he stayed true to himself by clinging to his creativity and making it his life's work.

At just twelve years younger than me, my niece Brooke, Sue's oldest, felt more like a sister to me. Always happy to please and bubbly, Brooke was a wonderful buffer to have in the presence of my father. Brooke's brother Darrell, Sue's youngest, was shy and as a boy looked a lot like his dad's family. He and Brooke always shared inside jokes, making me wish I had that kind of kinship with Sue. Her high school sweetheart turned husband, Bob, was also there. And, although he's a quiet, engineer guy and his conversations at the time consisted mostly of one-word responses: 'yep', 'no', I always felt like things would stay manageable in his presence.

Not surprisingly, there was a palpable awkward energy throughout the entire reunion. Dad kept trying to shuffle us all to be seated around a rectangular dining table in the hotel's restaurant. "I have something for each one of youuuu..." he exclaimed over and over again. His voice raised a few octaves as he drew out the "youuuuuuu." He was as excited as a little boy on Christmas Eve; except that he's a grown man, and Jewish and hated Christmas trees.

Thankfully, there were no other diners in the restaurant that day to witness our reluctance. It was better to receive Dad's weird presentation without an audience; knowing that his idea of gifts didn't quite match ours – to say the least. Our sibling rivalry kicked in as we secretly battled for the seats farthest away from Dad. Finally, when we were all seated, my dad pulled out a plastic bag, with the Hilton hotel logo on it, the kind they leave in your room for your laundry or swimsuit. I wondered if Kathy was fooled into thinking he had shopped at the Hilton gift shop.

I could practically hear the drumroll as he slowly reached his hand into the bag. All of us collectively held our breath, half expecting him to pull out a rabbit or a knife or a rabbit that had been knifed; who knew. Slowly, he pulled his hand out. In it was a two-sided cut out picture of Salvador Dali stapled together and attached to one of those huge tongue depressors. He actually had six of them, one for each of us.

What the...? This was weirder than anything I could have anticipated!

My siblings and I stifled our nervous laughter as Dad held up the Salvador Dali 'lollipop,' a Dali lolli; he launched into some story about how he and his lady friend, Rose, were traveling in Greece and went to a Salvador Dali exhibit where they handed these out. *Passing off free things as gifts was a gift he possessed. The less work he had to do to 'find' a gift, the better.* His eyes grew wide, a big grin stretched across his face, so pleased with his presentation and anxiously awaiting the gleeful response of his audience, us. Rose was a quiet woman, who, with her thin frame and hungry eyes, looked as though she always wanted that second offering of macaroni and cheese, but denied herself the indulgence. She had a slight blush to her face that I couldn't discern if it was embarrassment or withheld excitement. Personally, I was mortified. Here was a multimillionaire passing off shit he'd taken from hotels and museums as gifts to his adult children, when the only gift we ever desired was an apology for royally fucking up our lives. But if my father was nothing else, he was consistent, so I shouldn't have expected anything different from him. Yet there was always a part of me, deep down, that kept hoping.

Sitting there in the Stanley Hotel, my sisters, brother in-law, niece and nephew and I all side eyed one another, trying not to bust out laughing at the absurdity of it all. And Kathy, God bless her, throwing me a loving look as if she was hugging me with her eyes. On the way home she said, "Yep, your dad is pretty crazy."

I don't recall the drive home with Kathy, but I clearly remember the feeling I had. It was that of being trapped in a Dalí painting. Like time was melting and morphing into desert, into being deserted. An indeterminate time and space with a man who resembled my father, but had morphed into something else, something less scary and significant than I had previously thought him to be. Like pulling back the curtain on the Wizard of Oz to expose the small, aging, feeble man who would never be brave enough to expose himself.

CHAPTER 16

I knew I should've double-checked the definition of the word before I registered and showed up for class. But as I was scanning the Naropa University Continuing Education catalog and saw the title, "Curanderismo" I got a little 'ping' feeling, like an internal text alert saying, "you gotta take that class." I'd begun to pay more and more attention to that feeling. Since the time of Elijah, many continue to refer to it as the "still small voice of God". I prefer to think of it as a sort of spiritual text message.

Curanderismo is a traditional healing practice based on the belief that life is holistic: mind, body and spirit are the interconnected elements of life. Based on that perspective, all physical, mental, and spiritual illnesses are an imbalance of the mind-body-spirit; one cannot be separate from the other. The Spanish verb curar means to heal, it's the root and the essence of Curanderismo. Often referred to as Mexican American folk medicine, it dates back to the 1400s or even earlier to the Aztecs. Still prevalent today, Curanderismo continues to be part of a historically and culturally important health care system deeply rooted in native Mexican healing techniques.

My fingers were starting to freeze as they curled around the handlebars of my Sportster. *I should've worn heavier winter riding gloves*, I thought as I flipped the kickstand onto the pavement of Naropa University's Paramita campus lot. It was late September and, although I worried obsessively about my motorcycle sliding on piles of moist leaves, I loved riding it as late into the year as possible. I clipped my helmet onto my backpack and walked quickly towards the front door. *Damn, I should've looked at the map to see where my classroom was ahead of time.* There were others filtering into the building as well. *I'm not sure how to pronounce the name of the class... and I don't want to ask anyone for fear of sounding stupid for signing up for a class that I can't pronounce and didn't know what it was about but had a 'feeling' I should take it so...* I followed some guy who, although a few inches shorter than me and wearing a patch over one eye, seemed confident in where he was heading and hoped he would lead me to the right place. I was pleasantly surprised to see a man sitting cross-legged at the head of a circle of people sitting on cushions. He had brown skin and long black hair in a braid that nearly reached his waist. His features were welcome signs of diversity in the overwhelmingly whiteness of Boulder. He was our teacher.

The circle of twenty one students came to a sudden hush as our teacher began to speak. "I learned everything I'm about to share with you from my abuela, my grandmother," he said with both softness and command. There was an ease to him that naturally commanded respect. As he began to describe how he came to be seated in front of us, giving full credit to his maternal grandmother, a renowned Curandera, twenty one sets of eyes were transfixed on him. He spoke about being Mestizo, a man of Latin American descent, the son of a Spaniard and an American Indian.

Shedding my usual skepticism about spiritual stuff, I began looking forward to our class every Thursday evening. No two were the same and we always had homework. The most challenging for me was a project in which we were asked to make masks. One class in early November, our teacher said, "We all present masks to the world. This is an act of awareness and expression to depict your perspective of the face you show the world."

I whined and complained my way til Tuesday, when Kathy suggested I come to her house for help making my mask. Just then it dawned on me that, as an Art Therapist, Kathy couldn't be a more perfect fit for the task. Plus she knew me, possibly better than I knew myself, And she had an art studio in her home that was full of paints, glitter, glue and all things artsy. "I have simple paper mache masks you're welcome to use; or if you want to pick your own, you can get one at Michael's Arts & Crafts and bring it with you," Kathy said kindly on my voicemail. As we began working on my mask, my overwhelm was eased by her expertise. What I discovered was that underneath my anxiety was a vulnerability I was resisting. Not the actual exercise, but the fact that I had worn a mask my entire life; that the outside I presented to people was incongruous with my inside.

When it came time to present my mask to the Curanderismo class, I explained that I had decorated both the inside and outside of my mask; it had two sides. The outside of the mask wore a swath of yellow and orange, with happy birds on the corners of the eyes. The inside of the mask held swirls of black and the deep blue of storm clouds, streaks of red lightning and a pool of tears beneath the left eye. The outer portion represented the face I show the world and the inner, the face I keep to myself.

This wasn't the first class I'd taken in the Continuing Education Department at Naropa University. The summer semester prior to attending the Curanderismo class, I registered for a class called "Self Discovery in the Natural World". I thought it'd be like camping but for educational credit, and that perhaps, after completing this preliminary course I might continue to study in their new Wilderness Therapy Program. The class was co-led by a guy in his early thirties and a woman in her mid-fifties. Both white. The culmination of the nine-week class was a four day 'vision quest' in the San Juan mountains.

As my seven classmates and I hovered around a blazing fire on the eve of our vision quests, I thought, *I have no idea what I've gotten myself into*. We'd been told in a previous class that there would be a fire ceremony to, "melt resistance we may have towards the things in our lives around which we still were in need of healing."

In a soft tone, as if she was doing a voice over ad for maxi pads, our teacher, or 'guide' as she preferred, was describing how, when we abstain from eating food for four days, we become like pure vessels of nature. I had no idea what the heck that meant, let alone, whether it was something I aspired to. When I go without eating for four hours, I need some healing, so how the hell was I supposed to give up eating food for four days?

I excused myself, saying I had all the documents I wished to burn in my car (legal documents pertaining to my father as well as the stuff with that abusive boyfriend, Rich). With a flick of my hand and a half-hearted silent prayer, I tossed the thick manila envelope containing all the legal documents from both lawsuits into the fire. Watching the pages burn, words shriveling into ash, I hoped to never hear any of the following phrases again: *compensatory damages, demurrer,* and *malfeasance, domestic dispute, choking.* Gazing at the sparks and smoke, with my fellow classmates and our teacher/guide, I thought, *Shouldn't I feel something? Something more than just fascination with the flames?* There wasn't anything else I had to add, I knew that. And also knew that there was an entire bag of malted milk balls in my car, to keep me company on the drive home.

I left the fire for a moment, hopped into my car and started inhaling the tiny planets of chocolate with crunchy malt centers. I realized that the fear of not eating for four days wasn't the only thing gnawing at me... something didn't feel right about the whole ceremony. I kept wondering *what the fuck are these white people, including myself, doing?*

I sauntered back to the circle, trying to look serene. "Oh wonderful, you're back, Lisa," our 'guide' said, maintaining her maxi pad commercial voice.

After the fire, we were told to scout out a place where we'd stay for the next four days with only a tarp, a sleeping bag and water from the stream we could purify. I was grateful that I'd opted to bring a water purifier rather than iodine tablets. As I looked for my spot, my mind was filled with doubt and thoughts: *How will I know the 'place'? Am I just supposed to pick one?*

Just then, I turned to see the most exquisite view of the San Juans, the tips of the mountains with snow like icing on pointy cupcakes. Suddenly, in my mind, I heard my mom's voice singing, "white coral bells, along a slender stalk, lilies of the valley make my garden talk." It was a song we'd sing in rounds when piled into my mom's station wagon on road trips. I knew without a doubt that this was 'my spot'.

I set up my tarp tied to the base of a large blue spruce tree, whose trunk resembled a younger cousin of the giant redwood trees in California. Those of us 'vision-questing' were instructed to use a stack of stones in a formation called a 'cairn' to indicate whether we were okay or not. The 'guides' would be making rounds to check on our cairns to see if we'd placed the largest stone meant to be on the bottom of the stack, off to the side to indicate we were injured or needed something. Although I didn't question this system, I spent much of the first two days wondering if bears or other animals would mess with the rock towers.

On the third day, as the wind rippled through the nearby leaves like a soft breeze blowing a pinwheel, I sat on the dirt and rested my back against the bark. Suddenly all of my senses came alive, as if I'd been brought back to consciousness with smelling salts. The smell of malted chocolate balls filled the air. WTF?! But, really, the sweet smell wasn't coming from a box of chocolates, but from the sap of the tree I was resting on.

As my spine softened into the tree trunk, I felt the events of my life circling like the cells that form concentric circles inside trees. The rings indicate the amount of physical growth annually. I began to feel my hatred for my father dying. Like a gentle humming, all the good memories of my father began to encircle me: as a five year old in my favorite dress with the butterfly on the front, upset because we had to leave the petting zoo while Dad consoled me. Hummmmmmm. Dad explaining how the inner ear works before I had surgery to get tubes put in my ears. Hummmmmmm. The humming was fueled by sweet memories of my father. In the space where food would've filled me, I was getting nourished with feelings of tenderness towards my father.

Although I gained compassion and had a profound experience on that trip, I ultimately lacked guidance and understanding of the spiritual practice in which I participated. To this day I don't know how or if these two teachers were given the rights to guide and support others on vision quests. There was a thirst building in me I wasn't yet aware of. A thirst for authenticity, for learning, from those who've walked the talk.

According to Western Astrology, I was born under the sign of Sagittarius. True to form, I'll jump at any opportunity to travel and partake in any adventures about which I'm pretty clueless. That's how I ended up at Sacred Heart Ranch in Pryor, Montana for a Buffalo Harvest. I'd been invited by some friends of friends "to help harvest a buffalo for ceremony". It was early in the summer of 2005. The morning dew still held a frost, as if the chill of spring was having a difficult time letting go.

I'd be lying if I said I noticed the impish twinkle in his eyes, first. My eyes initially gazed at the rusty wheelchair that looked like it was dug out of a garbage heap; its blue vinyl back so cracked, I could see the grey threads barely supporting the weight of his torso. Perhaps it was the paradox of this junky wheelchair that made his sparkly eyes so pronounced. Nah, his eyes appeared to be in a perpetual state of planning another joke.

Long before I knew the phrase, 'the eyes are the doorway to someone's soul', I'd learned to search for the truth there. It's no coincidence that I shielded my eyes with a black baseball cap pulled low during my teenage years and early twenties before being steered towards a more honest path.

He knew I was scanning him for bullshit as he extended his big hand to shake mine. I've always been a sucker for hands. The kind that look like they can fix things, build stuff, pet dogs, hug kids, and still find time to cook a mean breakfast. Frank's hands fit the bill. They were a smooth reddish-brown showing, what I'd later learn, his Lakota and Cree heritage, and pre-arthritic knuckles like black knots on branches.

"Oh *there* you are!" He said, laughter just beyond his hand shake.

In any other circumstance, this statement by an older man, a stranger, would've made me say something snarky over my shoulder as I walked away.

"Uh, hi. We haven't met, have we?" I asked, my voice quivering.

I had just walked out of the humble ranch house at Sacred Heart to see this guy in a wheelchair taking a sip of iced tea he rested on the edge of a weathered picnic table.

His wide brown eyes responded to my question. No need for words. I sat down on the edge of the picnic bench, trying to keep my bare legs from touching the splintery wood. I had changed into my running shorts, hoping to release anxiety and unnamed emotions through the repetitive movement of my legs.

I like to consider myself fairly educated, for example, I wondered (silently) *why it wasn't referred to as a Bison Harvest; maybe be like harvesting berries or harvesting sage, which I'd done with folks who ran sweat lodges.* One of the native women taught me to offer a prayer of thanks and a pinch of loose tobacco to the earth before gathering sage. "And be sure to only harvest the male sage, the taller ones with wider leaves and no buds; take just a bit, never pull it up by the root so you're doing the sustain-able practice called 'wild crafting'. That way the plant will come back year after year and maintain it's indigenous integrity," she'd instructed in a firm yet gentle way.

But I didn't think about the fact that there'd be a gun involved in harvesting a buffalo. Or that getting my period the day before the harvest would preclude me from participating. To be honest, I was a bit relieved, even though I didn't fully understand. In native cultures, a woman menstruating, often referred to as 'being on her moon', was experiencing the most sacred of times, honoring the life giving quality held only by females. For most tribes, it was a ceremony in it's own right and not to be mixed with other cere-monies like sweats or sundances. I simply learned to respect and honor, even if I didn't fully comprehend.

When the harvesters returned to the ranch house that evening, they shared the extraordinary experience of how one buffalo stood out from the herd and literally offered itself for the harvest. And how, after a prayer then a single shot, the buffalo laid down, took its last breath and immediately was encircled by all the buffalo. They came up one by one, bowing their massive heads to touch noses with the deceased.

Frank asked if he could ride in my van for the drive to deliver the harvested buffalo to Porcupine, South Dakota for his relative's Sundance ceremony. Somehow I'd also missed that piece of the adventure, but like any decent Sagittarius, I said, "sure!" The van was my dream-van: a Ford E-350, 6.0 diesel van that had the interior of a Volkswagen Vanagon with a pop-up referred to as the 'penthouse'. Frank called it "a big red prayer tie," as he chuckled. The only downside was that we had to drive directly behind an old Chevy pickup truck, its bed full of ice packs... and the harvested buffalo. Covered with a large blue tarp bungeed to the side rails of the truck bed, one might not even know there was a huge carcass underneath, except for the trail of blood and water trickling constantly from the back right corner of the truck gate.

What should've been a six and a half hour drive took nine hours. The Chevy truck couldn't exceed 50 mph with the buffalo load. I poured my heart out to Frank; I told him all about my father murdering my mother and my struggles in my own relationships, most recently with Dakota, who happened to be one of the singers at the Sundance to which we were headed. Dakota and I had broken up (again, for the second time – out of what would be four total rounds together) a couple of months prior. It'd take me a number of years to see the truth that my gut knew from my first go-round in that relationship: Dakota didn't want a monogamous relationship but I chose to believe what he said, rather than trust my own intuition.

Frank was a proficient listener and offered his experience when I'd pause and glance at him in the passenger seat, "some men are always running from themselves. Do you know what I mean?" His eyes softened at me as he continued, "sometimes it takes a man like that a long time to learn the value and strength of a good woman and honor her. But unfortunately, a lot of men won't ever learn, and will live their entire lives running. Even as an old man, running in the mind."

I didn't know upon awakening that July morning, that later that day, I'd be receiving a whole new family and one of the greatest gifts of my life. On the second day of the Porcupine Sundance, Frank gave me tobacco and asked me to join him and his family at the tree. I didn't know why he was asking me, but I knew it was important. I'd met his extended family and marveled at the story Frank shared with me of how he'd found them. When Frank's father was on his deathbed decades ago, in a northern province of Canada, he finally told Frank that he had relatives in South Dakota. These relatives were descendants of Chief Iron Hail, Wasu Maza, the last survivor of the Battle of the Little Bighorn, also known as Dewey Beard. Frank's father told him nothing else and shortly after his passing, Frank traveled to South Dakota and began knocking on doors. At the Rosebud Reservation, people were sympathetic and eventually pointed him towards Pine Ridge Reservation. After many doors, he knocked on Mary Knoxnelly's door. The distance of decades and living in different countries dissipated as Mary, Beard's great-granddaughter and Frank's cousin, hugged him and said, "It's about time you got here, I've been waiting for you!"

Adjusting my shawl to be sure my shoulders were covered, I

entered the Sundance circle. I turned to honor the four directions and the Sundance tree as I'd learned to do. Mary Knoxnelly, her husband and their daughter and grandchildren greeted me with welcoming smiles as we stood beside Frank, sitting calmly in his wheelchair. He turned to look at me, "If it's alright with you, I'd like to adopt you as my daughter." His smile lit his whole face like a 20,000 watt bulb as he placed a bundle of tobacco bound in red cloth in my hands. As I nodded, tears dripped off my cheeks onto his hands that were holding mine.

To preserve the sanctity of what happened next, I'll only share that Frank requested a piercing ceremony. Piercing at the Sundance tree is very sacred and based on the belief that we have nothing but our own flesh and blood to offer the Creator. Flesh is offered in this way for prayers, for healing, for forgiveness, for gratitude.

"Not only have I adopted you," he looked at me the way I always wished my father would, "I've adopted all that comes with you: your family, your history, all of it. I'm going to pierce so that you and your family can be free.

CHAPTER 17

I was at least 50% fated to become a yogi.

An older woman named Antoinette was teaching yoga at a gym called Body Balance in downtown Boulder. Short and weighing less than 100 lbs, she had long dark hair and was wearing simple black yoga pants with a black top.

"Notice your breath," she said, "Your breath is the foundation from which all of the asanas originate". *Asanas?... Does she mean ass-in-the-air?* But there was no time to wonder, the class was already beginning to move and I was struggling to keep up. We did a few things that felt reminiscent of "head-shoulders-knees-and-toes-knees-and-toes" which seemed to be a warm-up for more challenging movements. "Ok, now inhale, your right leg high,"

Wait, how am I supposed to inhale my leg? High? How high? I'm sober!

Shit, behind again, I rushed to imitate what everyone else was doing.

"Now exhale," she said "Warrior Two. Virabhadrasana."

The word sounded beautiful to me although I had no idea what it meant. It resonated inside me and reminded me of my mom practicing arias for an upcoming opera. I always marveled at how she could sing in a multitude of languages: Italian, French, German; languages she couldn't speak fluently but sang with such passion as though it was her native tongue.

As I moved into the pose, I rolled my eyes and sighed heavily on the exhale. Not feeling at one with all living beings, I wasn't even feeling at one with my own being. I was feeling very inflexible: physically, emotionally and spiritually. *Was I the only one in the class breathing hard and sweating profusely?* I hated the quietness, the instruction to focus on my breath. I hated that I could hear the weights clanging in the room next door. To me, yoga had always seemed like a slow dance class, not a real workout. *What the hell am I doing here?* I thought, slogging through the rest of the confusing, contortionist hour.

My brother, sisters and I would poke fun at our mom, who practiced yoga long before it became popular. Standing in various postures while cooking or talking on the phone, I'd often catch her doing breathing exercises, especially when she seemed stressed or overwhelmed, which was often. One of her favorites was tree pose: standing on one leg, the foot of the other leg tucked high on the inner thigh of her standing leg. In hindsight, I see why that may have been her favorite posture - the need to be grounded in the midst of the constant chaos of our household. Had she learned that pose and its meaning from her yoga book that I took to Show and Tell years ago?

My personal journey towards yoga didn't begin in Antoinette's class; it actually began with weightlifting. I was introduced to lifting weights while rowing on the crew team at boarding school. It was a requirement at Emma Willard to participate in a sport; eating cookie dough wasn't considered a sport in anyone else's mind but mine, so I was forced to either play lacrosse or row crew. The notion of trying to run and toss a ball with what looked to me like a giant fly swatter seemed dreadful. I chose rowing.

Thankfully, our rowing coach at Emma Willard taught proper lifting technique. In order to maintain our conditioning over winter break, we made our own set of weights to take home:

two cement-filled coffee cans attached to one another with a broomstick. I bench pressed and squatted that Columbian coffee all winter break.

Six years later, I worked with a trainer in Chicago who taught me the basics of weight machines. Upon moving to Boulder, I joined a gym and worked out with a small, lean woman named Brenda who was a cross between a cheerleader and a Drill Sergeant. She never told me how much weight was on the bar and she always knew when my self-doubt kicked in. Laying on the weight bench with my hands on the bar, I would shake my head in disbelief: *Who the hell do I think I am trying to lift this, I'm the kid who never even passed P.E. in grade school!* Brenda would yell, "Don't shake your head! You gotta believe you can do it!" With no patience for negative thinking, she knew how important it was for me to discover my own mental and physical strength. So, I kept going to the gym and learned to tune out the negativity. I got strong. Really strong. Aware of my body changing, the gym became the one place where I really would try anything without being held back by doubt or fear. My abused, neglected body became a conduit for me to experience a sense of connectedness with myself and the world around me. I developed strong, healthy muscles on the outside and on the inside of my body.

I saw people doing yoga at the gym. After bench pressing more than my body weight, I would look over with sheer disdain between sets at the dimly lit yoga studio, full of bendy, mostly lanky women. Women contorted like hamsters in a cage, I couldn't, for the life of me, figure out the appeal of such a thing.

But after months of re-injuring my shoulder, I kept hearing, "You really should try yoga, it's the best way to heal." Continuing to resist their suggestions, the pain in my shoulder only increased.

One evening I finally snuck into the back of a class. There were more than a dozen people in the class, ranging in age from twenty to fifty-five. The room wasn't really a yoga studio, but rather a triangular shaped area with carpet that served as both the spin class and yoga room. When it was time for yoga, the spin bikes were lined along the back wall.

Walking to my car after class, something happened. I suddenly found myself breathing from my diaphragm. Not just my shoulder felt better, I felt better. For the first time, I felt good. Really good, different somehow, than I had ever felt. Completely present, in the moment.

After that first class I found another and another, discovering that I loved the simplicity of just focusing on my breath. Eventually, I loved trying to shape my curvy body into triangles. I loved that when I chose to, I could just breathe past all the competition, all the comparisons, all of my insecurities. Thirsting for an understanding of how and why yoga worked, I wanted to go to 'yoga school'. Nervously, I approached Brandon, one of my favorite teachers, "Can I sign up for teacher training even if I can't do a handstand and don't want to teach?" "Of course!" he kindly laughed. "Lots of people do the training just to learn more about yoga and expand their practice. You'd be a welcome addition to our upcoming training."

While I was becoming more and more at peace practicing yoga, I was becoming increasingly restless at work. I was so perplexed by my restlessness... a part of me felt like the demons of my experience were finally being transformed as I worked with and for a place that could possibly have saved my mother's life if she'd had access to a safehouse. But I also complained about aspects of it: I didn't get paid enough to work weekend events (not that

I necessarily had anything better to do), I hated having to carry a pager (a pager! That was so '90s), and our staff meetings every Tuesday were often long. Unless it was someone's birthday and then the length was quelled with cake. But the truth was, there was an undercurrent pulling me. Pulling me to share my story. I was beginning to realize that my experience and my loss empowered me to connect with others who have not felt safe in their own homes.

The mission of Safehouse included not only an emphasis on providing shelter and support for victims of abuse, but also addressing social justice issues like racism and white privilege. This was one of the things I loved about working for Safehouse. Knowing that if my father had not been a privileged M.D., he would've served a lot longer than six years in prison; I always knew that his whiteness was directly connected to him essentially getting away with murder.

CHAPTER 18

The word "transform" means to change a thing into a different thing. I had never trusted something that changed into a different thing.

As my wristband was scanned to enter Longhorn Hall, I noticed how the gal with long blonde hair held the scanner at a forty five degree angle to capture the barcode. It was Thursday evening, the first official night of the 2008 Yoga Journal Conference at Estes Park. I'd never heard of Matthew Sanford, the Keynote Speaker, but entrance to the Keynote was free for me as part of the Yoga Journal Work Study Exchange. Figuring there was much to learn in my first years as a yoga teacher, I was attempting to be the best sponge possible. My mind was full of questions, attempts to decipher acronyms and elements of language in this world of yoga.

One of the first things I learned is that the root of the word yoga in Sanskrit, the ancient language of yoga, is the word 'yuj' which means to unite. For me, the word "unite" evoked images of civil protests and rallies in front of the White House lawn. My family lacked any semblance of unity, rather, we lived with a daily fear of igniting my father's one-man explosions.

Sitting in the third row, slightly off stage left in Longhorn Hall, felt safer than in the front row, a bit off center enabled an easier exit if, after the first five minutes, I decided I'd rather go back to my bunk and rest. After all, my first work assignment was at 5 a.m. the next morning: hanging signs for the first day of the Conference classes. Although not one of those 'crack of dawn loving' yogi's, I looked forward to getting the lay of the land before the hoards of tight pants wearing, bendy people arrived. I watched the rows fill, surprised that only a handful of open seats remained. The moment Matthew Sanford began to wheel out onto the stage, the chattering crowd fell silent. His hands had a mastery of maneuvering his wheelchair, smooth, like painting. His body leaned distinctively to the left and the left side of his lips turned up in a slight smile, gaining some elevation lost by the rest of his body. I had arrived early, very unlike myself, and used the extra twelve minutes to read his bio:

"It took a devastating car accident, paralysis from the chest down, and dependence on a wheelchair before I truly realized the importance of waking both my mind and my body.

Matthew has explored yoga in a way that very few others ever have. His eighteen-year experience as a paralyzed yoga practitioner gives him an unprecedented perspective and he shares with people of all abilities – from the very advanced traditional student to the beginner with disabilities. His teaching challenges any student's perception of yoga, what it needs to look like and what it can be. For this, Matthew feels an enormous debt of gratitude to Sri BKS Iyengar. Without his revolutionary work with alignment, precision, emphasis on individual poses and innovative use of props, yoga would not be possible for Matthew."

I didn't care that it would be an hour wait to shake Matthew Sanford's hand and have him sign a copy of his memoir. I would have waited seven hours! Feeling the weight of his speech, the way he described moving his body, doing the yoga moves and making shapes that I often found hard to do, he described as having an ease and lightness.

Learning about his book: *Waking, A Memoir of Trauma and Transcendence*, was like finding a fortune tucked in the crevices of my heart. Matthew was the real, effing, deal!

Shaking his hand with a feeling of intimacy that far outweighed the moment, I felt the yuj, the uniting power of words. The words he used to share his story of being told, at age thirteen, that he should just forget about his lower body; those words that could've broken him, the same way his L7 vertebrae was severed, instead ignited a passion within him to find a way. Yoga paved that way, and little did I know, the man whose hand I wouldn't let go in that awkwardly long handshake, would become one of my most treasured yoga teachers.

I devoured the entirety of his book in one sitting. Following the Conference, I asked Matthew if I could study with him. He hadn't yet created a Teacher Training, but I asked if I could observe and assist classes and workshops he was teaching at his studio, Mind Body Solutions in Minnetonka, MN and at the Traumatic Injury Rehabilitation Center.

It took me years to concede that I felt a kinship with people who are differently abled. I had to first grapple with what felt like patronizing such a bond. I can reach the cookies off the top shelf at the grocery store without a thought and feel safe in my ability to cross a road in the length of time dictated by the stoplight. Eventually realizing although my losses didn't appear in the form of limbs or sight, I felt differently abled; an emotional paralysis Matthew Sanford shared: of being suddenly and traumatically altered emotionally, and for him, physically, at the age of thirteen.

From my first venture into yoga, I realized that beautiful

poses done by beautiful people, didn't interest me; I'm interested in what Matthew Sanford calls "the inside of yoga poses" and the ways to access those unseen aspects of yoga. My intrigue led me to study and earn certifications in Partner yoga, Restorative yoga, Sculpt yoga, Kundalini yoga, Yin yoga, StandUp Paddleboard yoga, and Sanskrit, the ancient language at the heart of the practice. My curiosity and connection to this unfolding world resided deep inside of me.

Learning that each sound in the Sanskrit alphabet lights up a particular spot in our physiology, and simultaneously connects to an element of nature, I thought, "My mom would've loved this." Sanskrit is the confluence of two things she loved: language and energetics. Together we had created a big binder with a colorful page for a new word each day to enhance my vocabulary. As a writer, Mom had an intimate relationship with words; she would foster new words as if they too were her children.

With closed eyes, she would open the dictionary at random and put her finger on her new 'baby'. She'd always opened her eyes to exclaim, "Welcome, word!" and then nurture it throughout the day, inviting it into as many opportunities and conversations as possible.

I wasn't quite as fond of this game, as for me it was more a vicarious delight. What I really relished was the time spent with her. With four kids, a dog, three guinea pigs, a house, a difficult husband, and all her creative interests, her time was a priceless commodity.

There were many moments in my yoga studies when I'd have that thought: *my mom would've loved this!* There were other moments when I'd learn something that seemed to be the missing puzzle piece for which I'd forever been searching. Sometimes a memory would surface as I moved through the physical practice of asanas. These moments were crystal clear and transported me to the time and place which it occurred. Once while holding pigeon pose, my right shin resting on my mat, my right knee in line with my right hip, my left leg outstretched behind me, I bowed my chest to rest on my right leg, and touched my forehead to my mat. I suddenly felt this moment:

Mom looked straight at me, her green eyes serious but the corners of her eyes crinkled, she called them her "smile lines". They lightened up the moment. She held her right pinky up to link with mine, alerting me to a forthcoming pinky pact.

"I want you to promise me that that you will choose love over fear. Promise me you'll always take the 'high road' and that you won't despair in the face of disappointment, you won't retaliate when offended. Pinkypromise me."

Dang Mom, that's a lot to promise, I tried to bargain. "You can do it," her right eyebrow lifted as if to challenge me.

I marveled how, despite her busyness and the constant chaos of her relationship with my dad, she managed to write little notes on our lunch bags or slip them in our backpacks. I saved every single one of my notes from her, which is a strange thing for a kid to do.

Did I already tell you that?

Do you already know about the notes? Does it matter if I tell you again? Those notes are time travelers. Those notes make me feel connected to my mother. Those notes remind me of my pinky promise.

Somewhere in me, I knew my time with her would be fleeting.

Each note was unique: some were written in a circle, so I had to turn the page all the way around multiple times to read the entire thing. Others had pictures or stickers. My favorite note, now so worn it's barely readable:

" You are the light of my life.
I'm so glad you're my baby.
I love you more than words can say."

In my first Yoga Teacher Training, we learned about Ujjayi Pranayam. It's a pattern of breathing typically practiced in Hatha Yoga, in which you inhale and exhale through the nose. It's typically translated to mean "victorious breath" with the explanation that what we have victory over are the fluctuations in our minds, or our incessant thoughts. Ironically, upon hearing this, I began to have incessant thoughts about the word 'victory' and my mom's headstone.

There was no headstone for over a year after her death; my dad wanted her to be buried in New York state, beside her parents who were buried in Dunkirk, the tiny town near Buffalo where my mom grew up. My dad had ordered a headstone that was to read:

"Mary Ellen Ruth Bailey Fierer
Beloved wife, and mother
May she rest in peace"

Although 'merely' twelve, as frequently reminded by the Defense Attorney and Judge presiding over the case, I took every measure to express my vehement opposition to my father having any say whatsoever in our mom's tombstone. As he was attempting to control from behind bars, the community at Hopedale Church where Mom, Jonny and I had spent Thanksgiving, had already ordered a temporary headstone. The inscription would haunt me for years. It read:

"You've got the Victory!"

A few years later, while midway through a six month Kundalini Yoga Teacher Training, practicing the mantra 'Wahe Guru Wahe Jio' in a sea of trainees all wearing white, I experienced a complete transformation. Wahe Guru Wahe Jio is used as a meditation to shift from fear to love. "Wah" is a divine spiritual, wonderful wow. "He" means here and now. "Guru" means from what is dark may light prevail. "Jio" means soul. This mantra is often referred to as a 'victory song'.

While many consider a mantra to be a slogan or motto, it's meaning comes from the combination of the (Sanskrit) root words "manas" and "tra". "Manas" is described as the 'place' in which the heart and mind align, and "tra" is the emanation or outer expression of that heart/mind center.

The place where my mother and I aligned in heart and mind was expressed through our pinky pacts. Unknowingly, she was teaching me the foundation of Wahe Guru Wahe Jio, our secret victory pact: no matter what life slung at us, we would choose love, we would prevail.

CHAPTER 19

In the still cool nights of late April in Colorado, 2007, I slept in my big red van parked outside of the yoga studio where I taught an 8 a.m. class. Well, it wasn't really that I spent the night. About 2 a.m. that morning, I had checked my boyfriend Dakota's cell phone and discovered what I'd been suspecting all along- that he had been exchanging highly inappropriate pictures with multiple women when he was presumably in a committed relationship with me. I began shouting at him, "Why don't you just fucking ride off on the high horse you think you came in on," I yelled, not even sure what the hell I meant. He slammed the apartment door. I think it's progress that I chose someone who slammed the door instead of me. But, still...The slam of his apartment door swallowed up the sound of his response- if he had one.

Driving away, my body felt like a sweater with one loose thread, completely unraveling. I'd learned by now that it's best to pull to the side of the road when sobbing. Especially the body wracking sobs. It was something much deeper than the loss of my relationship with Dakota driving my emotions. But all I could see at the time was that living was simply too painful. Through the haze of my water filled eyes and my Sportsmobile headlights, I saw a bridge just about five meters ahead. It had old wooden rails, the kind that would be easy to barrel through with my one ton vehicle. As I glanced in my rearview mirror to see if there were any headlights, something red caught my eye. I turned around and realized it was an anklet made of sage and wrapped in red cloth reflecting light from the back seat.

"Burn this when you need strength, when you don't know what else to do, the power of these prayers and this ceremony will come to you." I remembered Tom saying to me as he handed me one of the anklet's he danced with for four days in Montana at Sundance. Although I hadn't yet met him, he caught my eye the first day of the dance. Even from a distance of ten yards, he had the distinct vibe of trouble. Over the next four days, I watched him transform from a thug to a man infused with, shall I say, spirit. The hardness melted, perhaps from dancing under the harsh August sun, along with the humbling effects of starvation and thirst. He became such a clear example for me of the transformative effects of a sacred commitment. I shared that with him at the end of the dance when I went to thank him for dancing and offered to help him pack up his tent and belongings.

Pulling onto the shoulder, I lit an exposed sage leaf sticking out from one end of the anklet with the cigarette lighter in my Sportsmobile. As the red cotton cloth and sage burnt, it was as if the smoke began to quickly knit my unraveled self back together. The urge to drive off the side of that bridge was gone. In its place was gratitude for my life and the knowledge that the pain I felt in this moment would pass. Deciding to simply park in front of the yoga studio and catch a couple hours of sleep before teaching; this thought came to me from somewhere other than my own mind, *"there may be someone in a worse place than you who needs to come to a yoga class to find a reason to keep living."*

A heavyset woman came up to me after that class. I couldn't tell if it was tears or sweat on her face as she said to me in a low voice, "Even though I'm not very good at yoga, this class saved my life, thank you," her pale blue eyes looked into mine, "My husband left me last night and I laid awake telling myself to just keep breathing until 8 a.m. yoga."

Four days later I was checking in to a five-day Breakthrough Inpatient Program at Caron Treatment Center outside of Wernersville, Pennsylvania. My friends, Cathie and her husband Paul, had let me stay at their house in the woodlands of Nederland, Colorado for the four days following my close call of almost driving off the bridge. Not wanting to acknowledge that I had been suicidal, I couldn't deny that what used to feel like solid bones in my body, now felt like flimsy tubes of water. Although spared with a moment of reprieve in my van, I was by no means well. It would take me a few more years before piecing together that the despair I felt at the end of a relationship was rooted in the trauma of losing my mom. Cathie suggested looking into the Breakthrough Program at Caron Treatment Centers. Pulling up their website, I read,

"If you're struggling to connect with others, feel joyful or flourish in general, Breakthrough Caron might be right for you. Our innovative program has helped thousands of adults pursue self-improvement, see themselves clearly for the first time and realize their desires for happy, fulfilling lives."

I sure as shit was struggling to feel joyful. And definitely in need of a healthy emotional breakthrough rather than breaking through the loose planks of a wooden bridge. I kept reading,

"Using experiential techniques that gently bypass natural defenses and raise awareness of feelings and attachments, Breakthrough groups focus on how to live rather than life's problems. Every aspect of Caron Breakthrough presents an opportunity for healing and personal growth in an intimate, therapeutic group setting. No time is wasted."

I sat nervously on the edge of an uncomfortable wooden chair off to the side of the Intake Therapists desk. As he was filling out the first two lines of paperwork, I noticed how similar his profile looked to a photo of my father when he was a medic in the Air Force. I thought mentioning it might break the ice a bit.

"Let's get one thing straight," his voice was crisp as he turned to face me, "I am not your father." Though I was hoping for more of a Star Wars' bonding moment, no time was wasted in bypassing my natural defenses! The five days I spent at Caron proved to be far more than they'd promised.

All I remember was that the promise seemed gentle on the website, like a warm hug, like cookies baking in an oven, but it was intense. That's all I remember: the tension between the 'gently bypassing' and full-steam ahead.

Six months later, I'd be putting the lessons learned there to the test and hoping to cash in on their healing dividends.

"Lis?" Robin asked rather than stated.

"Yeah – hi Wobbie" (affectionate nickname from childhood when I couldn't pronounce 'r's).

"Lis, I gotta tell you something... you're not driving or anything are you?"

"No, I'm in my pj's in my kitchen. Rob, what is it?"

"Lis, Dad's dead."

"Whoa. Are you serious?"

I dropped to my knees onto the kitchen floor of my loft in downtown Boulder.

"Holy smokes. How? Oh my gosh, oh my gosh"

I began sobbing, filled with shock and disbelief.

"Lis, I know, honey. He had a heart attack early this morning."

"Oh my God. Oh my God."

All of a sudden, I hear Billy Joel singing in my head: "Heartattackackackackack"

"Wow Rob. What do we do?"

"I don't really know. I've gotta call Sue and Jonny."

"Ok. You want me to call Jonny?"

"Sure."

In true Fierer fashion, we kept talking even after we had once, twice, nearly three times ended the conversation. Robin and I tried to figure out what you're supposed to when your dad dies, where was the guidebook for such an event? Robin suggested, "let's dial a Jew for advice." I agreed, there's probably protocol to follow for the death of a Jew but, since we were only intermittently Jewish, we were both unsure.

We bantered back and forth, relying on the saving grace of humor, "What would a Jew do?"

"Oh, we really do need a Jew...we don't know what to do...."

After healing giggles, we professed our sisterly love for one another and promised to call each other later. That's the thing about death, how even in the darkness of loss, a light shines on the preciousness of each moment.

The plan was that Robin and I would fly to Florida the next day and stay with Tiffany, dad's girlfriend of five years (she came after the skinny-but-starving Rose at The Shining hotel). We both knew Tiffany but Robin had spent much more time with her than I had. Jonny would join us the day after and stay a few days longer to help clean out Dad's apartment.

I don't remember where Sue was, is that weird? But she wasn't there.

The day Robin and I arrived at Tiffany's was Thanksgiving, 2007. I'd been single for much of my adult life, sprinkled with a number of disastrous relationships, yet I found strange comfort in my father's connection with Tiffany. After meeting her briefly, I knew Tiffany was the female version of my father complete with qualities of being narcissistic, condescending, temperamental, conceited and pessimistic. I reckoned, if they had found one another, there had to be hope for me finding a mate.

That afternoon, Robin and I went to Starbucks for our daily fix and to escape Tiffany's pestering to sit down and write an obituary. We were standing in line behind a police officer, commiserating about our circumstances, when all of sudden, Robin turned to the officer and said, "Officer, could you please arrest me? I would much rather be in jail right now." My chin dropped in disbelief, as did the barista's. I thought the officer might actually arrest her for making fun of the severity of his civic duty, but he just smiled and got that shielded look like he'd dealt with many types of people in his line of business.

As the day's events continued, Robin and I became prisoners of sorts. After a fairly successful Thanksgiving dinner out at a seafood restaurant on the Pier, Tiffany wanted to go by Dad's place and get some of her stuff, check his answering machine and mail. Robin, sat in the backseat of Tiffany's car as we silently signed to one another using a thumbs up or thumbs down system to determine who had enough patience to ride in the passenger seat with Tiffany driving. Robin said sadly, "I don't want to go to Dad's place on Thanksgiving." Tiffany just kept rambling on and on, but I believe she did hear Robin's request. She pulled up to Dad's apartment complex and parked.

"Are you fucking kidding me?" the sadness had fled Robin's voice, replaced with burning rage. "I said, I don't want to go to Dad's today, it's Thanksgiving," her face was hotter than sidewalk

cement on an August day. "What part of that didn't you understand Tiffany?" Spit flew out of Robin's mouth as she said Tiffany's
name. I held my breath waiting for Tiffany's response.

"Well, Robin. I understand. But it's on the way and we really
need to check his mail and answering machine. There are people
who may not know he's passed and are expecting to hear from
him," her tone condescending, eerily familiar to my dad's. "We
don't always get what we want Robin."

I clenched my butt anticipating the impending emotional
explosion. In a show of sibling support, I sat in the car with Robin
while Tiffany went inside our father's apartment. As soon as
Tiffany angrily slammed the car door, Robin began to sob silently:
a prisoner in Tiffany's backseat. I unclenched my ass. For some
reason it didn't bother me to be at Dad's on Thanksgiving, but I
felt compassion for Robin's sensitivity. And even some compassion for Tiffany – that narcissism, much like our dad's, seemed to
deafen her ears and her heart.

Returning to the car, Tiffany said something that couldn't be
more true, nor more foreshadowing.

"For all I know, he had a double life."

Monday morning following Thanksgiving weekend, we
had a day of meetings with Dad's lawyers and financial officers
in charge of his estate. I was still waiting for the airlines to find
and deliver my luggage lost upon my arrival four days earlier. If
I had considered this possibility, I would have chosen to wear a
different outfit. I sported a miniskirt made out of old army fatigue
pants, bedazzled with rhinestones (cuter than it sounds), a black
spandex halter top and black flip flops. At least it was weather
appropriate for South Florida.

I became acutely aware that my attire was slightly out of

place at the UBS office. Jonny, Robin and I were escorted into the Board Room; I tried to tuck myself and my awkward outfit behind them. The receptionist indicated for us to have a seat at the extraordinarily large, oval-shaped, conference table with plush seats that made us feel like little kids when we sunk into them. Then an entourage of brokers entered, clad in three piece business suits, cuff-links and gold pinky rings. As I stared down at my thighs, marveling at how much shorter my mini-skirt was when seated, I wondered if this was how Julia Roberts felt in *Pretty Woman.*

Feigning mild interest as they recited their Bios, and what felt like a sales-pitch, I wondered what they might be selling and if this was the nature of these types of meetings. I began to pay attention when Jack Hughs, my father's attorney, introduced himself. He's the guy who represented my father in the legal action I'd pursued to get him to be accountable for the funds he'd hidden and essentially embezzled. Trusting a guy like that would be inherently questionable. He looked uncannily like Santa Claus: white beard, smiling blue eyes and red cheeks. I wasn't considering sitting on his lap, especially not in my miniskirt, but I did have to fight the urge to hug him when he introduced himself. To his credit, Hughs was just doing his job, representing my dad, which could not have been an easy task. My heart continued to soften when he professed, "Josh (my dad) was the tightest person I know." A few days later I would find out what Hughs meant.

What is the point of this meeting? Was it strictly protocol for the financial team of the deceased to meet with next of kin? Maybe if I'd focused less on my mini-skirt, I would've garnered a deeper understanding.

Jack Hughs did read our father's will. Surprisingly, I wasn't admonished entirely from it, as I presumed from the court settlement of my lawsuit against Dad. He had kept me in his Will, but true to form, the money he'd 'left' for me was secured in a Philanthropic Fund. Meaning, he only left me money that I could donate, essentially in his name.

Five days later, I was standing in front of another door not wanting to enter. The oversized wooden door at the entrance of Palms West Funeral Home was formidable, yet strangely inviting and looked like a doorway to a temple. I paused with my hand on the gold colored handle, expecting the weight of the door to match it's appearance. It practically opened by itself. I peered up to see the hydraulic metal openers at the top of the twelve foot door frame. Inside, the décor reminded me of Grandma Poppi's living room: a gold textured console table that held the Guest Registry and to the right, a set of space filling sofas not for sitting on. I was ushered to sit in the front row on one of the hard wooden pews lining the room for the commemorative service. As I contemplated rearranging the furniture so I could sit on a sofa, our Rent-a-Rabbi arrived.

Robin and I had determined that we definitely needed a Rabbi for Dad's memorial service. A non-orthodox Rabbi, particularly since we didn't know if Dad had been going to a Synagogue during the time he lived in West Palm, Florida. And perhaps even more importantly, because the body is traditionally considered the property of God and it's forbidden to defile the body; some consider the willful burning of human remains such an act of dishonoring. The irony was not lost on me that we had to make such considerations for a man who had committed defiling atrocities on his wife.

Robin and I made call after call trying to find a Rabbi available for hire so close to Thanksgiving. Rabbi Joshua Levine was our only option at $500 for a maximum of forty-five minutes. It sounded like a more profitable profession than prostitution. He seemed decent enough over the phone and showed up wearing a yarmulke and with what we hoped would be the appropriate Hebrew prayers.

I was sitting at the end of the pew in the front row next to my Cousin Susan who'd flown in from Maine, Robin sat beside her. Jonny positioned himself by the exit due to a sudden bout of explosive diarrhea. A minute before the service began, the Rabbi made his way down the row, shaking our hands and giving condolences. I was last and thought I must be imagining things when, as he shook my hand, he didn't look at my face as he had with Cousin Susan. Instead he looked directly at my chest. After he walked away, I too stole a glance at my chest, but only to make sure my breasts were appropriately concealed. My luggage had finally arrived so at least for this parent's funeral, I was able to wear my own black dress.

I leaned over to Susan, whom I loved from the moment she arrived, to ask if she had seen what just happened. A smirk instantly formed on her lips, "Maybe he'll discount the bill!" I smiled and leaned in a little closer, wishing she'd have been there for us after my mom died. I don't doubt she would have, if she'd known the truth.

After the service, a woman named Bobbi, her face coated in foundation a few shades too light, shook my hand like she'd waited her whole life to meet me. Her eyes were filled with tears and I hoped she'd chosen waterproof eyeliner and mascara. Still holding my hand, Bobbi began to tell me how she lives, "lived," she corrected herself, the tears now cascading down her cheeks, with a landfall of makeup in the mix, in the same apartment complex as my father. Though she'd never seen my father's children visit, she knew how much he loved kids. Curious, I let my hand remain in hers, wondering if she had come to the wrong funeral. Bobbi continued, telling me that she was raising her grandson, who had his bicycle stolen; someone broke the lock, he was devastated. "Outside our home, can you imagine?" she asked rhetorically. Apparently, my dad helped them look for the stolen bike, sadly, to no avail. "A few days later, Josh showed up at our door with a Brand New Bicycle," she overly annunciated those last words. "And..." Bobbi paused dramatically, "he swore me to secrecy. He's so humble that he didn't want to take credit."

Could it be that there are two funerals with two different 'Josh's'? I wondered.

I felt a flash of anger.

As kids, my siblings and I, and even our mom, had to beg and plead for money for necessary school stuff. Not because of a lack of money, it was about power and control. And here, my father angelically splurged for some random kid.

Using my 'inside voice,' I silently ranted in my head. Meanwhile, my hand was still held by Bobbi's and my head nodding, a smile accessorizing my face.

I realized at that moment, that perhaps nothing is black and white, that this is the grey matter so to speak. That everyone, even my father, is multifaceted. And, I had no right to try to make Bobbi see what a monster my dad had been, she was entitled to her own experience with my dad, her grandson's bike angel. As Bobbi finally released my hand, I thought how sad it must have been for my father to do for others what he could not do for his own family.

There is an extraordinary amount of paperwork in the wake of a death. At least that's how it was with my father. I had frequented the Notary at my local bank and, still afraid of any one person knowing too much about me, I decided to branch out. I visited the Wells Fargo downtown location and waited patiently, flipping through my day planner, until I was greeted by Barbara.

As she shook my hand, I tried not to stare at all of the mini-mogul like bumps on her face. At about sixty, she was far too old for acne, but spunky enough to ask me more than fifteen minutes worth of questions. I suppose as a "Guarantor" of my signature, she felt it was important to know all about me, my life and every-thing leading up to these three papers I had asked her to notarize.

"My father passed away in November and this is, I believe, the last of the paperwork to be signed, so that the title to his car can be turned over to the new buyer." *Sucker,* I thought silently; *my dad had to replace the clutch three times in this second hand Nissan he bought and he put a USAA sticker over the dent on the right front bumper rather than get it repaired.*

"Oh, darling, you're so young to lose your father. I hope you're close with your mother."

"Well, she passed away when I was really young."

"Oh, my you're an orphan!" she exclaimed, loud enough for the whole bank to hear.

No one had ever acknowledged that I lost both parents, and essentially my entire family as I knew it, when I was twelve. Police, Guardian Ad Litem, Judges, Lawyers, no one. Somehow, we were unnoticed, unrecognized, and unnamed orphans. At that moment I realized I was hearing validation twenty three years too late.

But my perspective was transforming: I could now see that people had been so freaked out by my dad killing my mom, that they just didn't know what to do. Perhaps they did the best they could and in my grief and overwhelm, I couldn't acknowledge their efforts. Walking out of the bank and onto the brick walk of the Pearl Street Mall, I thought *perhaps my experience could help others.*

Two days later while surfing the Internet, I googled "children who have lost a parent to Domestic Violence". One find popped up. *When does only One find pop up from a Google search?*

I clicked on the link.

A huge lump formed in my throat as I began to read Dr. Barbara Parker's five year study of adults who, as children, lost a parent(s) to a fatal act of domestic violence. Oh my God. I found my people. There's a fifty-three minute audio link of her presentation at the Vera Institute of Justice. I listened to the whole thing in one sitting, and downloaded the power-point presentation and followed along.

One slide had a single word, "Uxoricide". I never heard this word... Dr. Parker quoted Webster's definition, "murder of one's wife; can refer to the act itself, or the man who carries it out."

Holy shit.

This happens and has happened enough that there's a word to describe what I've survived.

Dr. Parker cites that approximately twice as many children are affected by Uxorcide than Leukemia. I've certainly heard about Leukemia. Why not Uxoricide? And I've lived through it... what if I'd survived Leukemia, without even being diagnosed or able to talk about it?

CHAPTER 20

I never would've thought that learning an ancient language would lead me back to something I'd lost.

I balanced my left toes on the edge of the highest shelf, my right hip smashed into the plywood wall of my storage unit. Most people would use a ladder, but I enjoyed the thrill of my amateur climbing and risk taking to scale the four-foot wide, twenty feet high space the Pearl Street Lofts Association optimistically called, "generous storage space with each unit". I reached both of my hands to the shelf above and pulled down the unmarked box that had caught my eye. I opened the mysterious box, looking for the series of letters my father and I had written to one another just a few months prior to his sudden death. As I sliced through the packing tape, I thought about how annoyed I'd been when I opened my father's first letter and out fell a photocopy of my letter to which he was responding. He always built a case for his perspective, long before he earned a law degree during the time he was incarcerated. My dad would use newspaper articles and anything necessary as 'evidence' for the points he was making. It was particularly maddening to have my words highlighted and used to his advantage.

When I saw what was inside the box, I gasped so deeply, my lungs filled in a way they'd only done as a teenager doing 'whip-pits' inhaling on empty canisters of Whip Cream. Only this time, instead of delighting in that light-headed feeling, I fell to my knees on the cold concrete storage room floor. The box was filled with cassette tapes from my mom's singing lessons over three decades ago. I pulled each one out as if handling a newborn baby, carefully untangling the analog magnetic tape that had unraveled from many of them. I wondered if I could salvage them by sticking a pencil eraser in the tape reels like we used to do in middle school. Then it occurred to me that I didn't even own a tape player.

Two weeks later I was sitting on the floor of my living room, twisting bits of shag rug between my fingers as my ears drank in the familiar sounds of a voice I hadn't heard in twenty-five years.

My mom's voice.

My friend Cathie Soderman recommended I call a musician friend of hers, Tom Wassinger, to salvage and digitize my mom's cassette tapes. Every turn on the winding drive up Sugarloaf Mountain to meet Tom made me question what I was doing. But when I arrived, his kindness soothed my doubts as he showed me around his home studio, describing all the instruments lining the walls. When it came time to hand over my mom's tapes, my fingertips were turning white from gripping the box so intensely. Without any explanation on my part, Tom gently took the tapes from me, his blue eyes grasping the depth of meaning in this musical exchange.

Twisting the rug gave me both a sense of grounding, and something tangible. The tape played and I heard my mom's voice say,

"Lisa, sweetie, please don't run your matchbox car on the side of the piano. Can you take it over there?"

A jolt of forgotten recognition traveled through my ears into my heart, hearing my mom's voice after two and a half decades. And then I heard my four year old voice say, "okay Mommy, but it's not a car, it's a truck."

I couldn't have predicted how useful my early exposure to hearing foreign languages and intonations would be to learning Sanskrit, the foundational language of Yoga. "When we travel to a country that's foreign to us, one of the first things we do is learn a bit of the language. Language becomes a bridge to one another," I listened intently as my Sanskrit teacher, Manorama spoke.

The irony is that my bridge to learning Sanskrit was paved with impure motives. Sanskrit wasn't included in my first 200 hour Yoga Teacher Training. As my group of teachers in training practiced teaching, it became clear to me how much I sucked: I talked too much, too quickly, and cared too much whether the students thought I was interesting and funny. I heard about an afternoon workshop called Sanskrit for Yoga Teachers. *That's it!* I thought, *If I learn how to pronounce the names of the postures in Sanskrit, I'll at least sound like I know what I'm doing.* When I heard the opening chant to the workshop, it felt like a vibrational love letter. Two years later, when I received my Sanskrit teacher's blessing to begin teaching under her tutelage, I'd share that the way I came to be sitting in front of them was that I had been seduced by Sanskrit. Like a lifelong love affair, I became more and more intrigued with every nuance I'd learn: how many of the sounds and their meanings relate to Lakota, Cree, Hebrew and other languages. These connections are what Manorama calls "following the sutras" or the threads of connection. For example, the English word, "suture" has its roots in the Sanskrit word, "sutra": the literal threads that are used to stitch a wound together. But deeper curiosity suggests that the translation includes the experience of 'su', meaning good or well. It's this state of good-ness that is available through the healing of a break (physical and/or emotional).

Translating is always deep and multifaceted, however, the way I learned Sanskrit was not without wit and a sense of light-heartedness. For example, I learned that the Sanskrit word 'Guru', often defined as, " teacher", consists of two elements: 'gu' (goo) meaning darkness and 'ru'(roo) meaning light. Manorama shared, "whatever ru's your gu is your Guru". Whatever person or situation ruffles your feathers has the most to teach you.

One of the guru's I resist the most is discipline. I loathe the repetition of a predictable schedule and yet I know because of my resistance that's precisely what I need. After graduating from an 18 month intensive Yoga for Sanskrit Teachers course I enrolled in another course to learn the Sanskrit chants that correspond to the phases of the moon, called the Shri Suktam. When we were given the assignment to practice the Shri Suktam nine times each day for twenty seven days to total 108, a number weighted with spiritual significance, I made it nine days. Three days later, I couldn't tolerate the feeling of failure. I paused, sat still in meditation which led to a new commitment: I would chant the Shri Suktam once a day for 108 days. I completed that obligation, most days before sunrise, the time of day considered to be the most auspicious time for such a practice. Auspicious. A word my mom would've loved. *Most favorable for success, prosperous.*

During those years insomnia plagued me, the only chance I had of getting sleep was the pre-dawn hours from 3 a.m. until about 7 a.m. At that time, something in me succumbed and in what are said to be the darkest hours, I discovered an innate source of light. My Sanskrit practice gave me a sense of strength beyond what I could achieve in the gym.

Fifty-four days into my Shri Suktam practice, in the fall of 2009, I had a dream in which my mom was singing opera while

I chanted. In many of my dreams, I only recall pieces and they quickly fade. But this dream remained clear. It didn't make sense at the time, but I knew what I had to do.

I drove the road up Sugarloaf Mountain to Tom Wassinger's for a second time. Although not anxious the way I had been the first time, I felt nervous to have him record my chanting. I didn't want something that felt so sacred to succumb to the possibility of becoming performative. Tom assured me, "just begin when you'd like and I'll stay back here." We met a few more times during which Tom added instrumentals. Not virtual instruments, but one of the plethora lining the walls of his studio. He and I would marvel at the synchronicity that kept appearing as we spliced the excerpts of my mom singing into my chanting the Shri Suktam. A musician, producer and Nammy Award winner, Tom was excited to be working on something that had never before been done. He had recording software that enabled him to slow down the recordings as well as change the key in which my mom was singing, even draw out one continuous note. As Tom played some of those examples for me, it was as though my mom's voice had come to life but was trapped in a place in which I couldn't see or touch her. In that moment, it felt as though she'd been alive all along, searing my heartstrings in a way I almost couldn't bear. Most of the pieces salvaged from my mom's recordings were in other languages, but when Tom played the slowed down version of this particular piece sung in English, we both gripped the edges of the recording studio stools.

> "you are no longer one of us
> depart at once
> and leave this house"

To grieve someone over the course of a lifetime is to sing with the dead. When we lose someone, our arms ache wanting to hug them or our fingers may pause when we reach for our phone to call. But they show up, in memories, in dreams, to sing with us. We carry their disembodied voices with us always.

Perhaps what my mom sought solace in—the power of using your voice as a vehicle for healing expression—is what I was learning in my Sanskrit and chanting practice. I'd begun to see that each of us has the choice in any given moment to use our voices for good.

CHAPTER 21

Every time I attended a Sundance ceremony with Frank, whether it was in Montana, South Dakota or Canada, I remember thinking, *there's no way in hell I'd ever aspire to do That.* Four days with no food and no water, dancing from sunrise to sunset, in hopes that my prayers were meaningful through such suffering. As Sundance supporters, Frank and I (along with many others) were there to share our strength, prayers and gratitude to the dancers for their sacrifice and commitment. Frank was one of the revered Elders at these ceremonies and he taught me through his actions and gentle guidance to think of the dancers every time I had a drink of water or ate anything. I didn't understand at first, but have begun to glimpse that there's some unseen web of connection that exists between everybody and everything. This web is much like the deeply connected root system that's shared by all the trees in the aspen grove that lined my first four days as a Sundancer.

It was 2011 when I got the call. My sister Robin had given birth to my niece, Gianna Mary (her middle name after our mom), whom we'd already begun to refer to as Gigi. From the time I was seven years old, I remember Robin desperately wanting a baby of her own. I guess that's a phase a lot of kids go through, but for Robin it never passed. Not knowing yet the intricacies of baby-making, I said to her, "RaRa, if ever you can't have a baby, I'll have one for you, k?"

Much like actually having a baby is far more involved than simply wanting one, I was beginning to learn that becoming a Sundancer is a tremendous commitment. I first needed to ask for permission to dance from the Sundance Leader. So I presented him with tobacco, shared my reason(s) for dancing, and answered many questions from him, not the least of which was, "what's going to make you keep your commitment when everything in you wants to quit?" He then took my responses and pledges of commitment with him to prayer and proceeded to give me specific instructions on how to prepare myself.

As a white woman, I am aware that the invitations and welcome I've received to participate at any level in native ceremonies are an honor not to be taken lightly. I've heard it said that whatever we are grateful for, we are responsible to; I take this to heart. For those reasons, it's not appropriate for me to share the intricacies and protocols of these ceremonies outside a few of the particulars as they relate to my personal experience.

Even though I had completed the necessary Hanbleceya, crying for a vision or dream as it's called in Lakota, it seemed nothing could have truly prepared me for my experience as a first year Sundancer. Every hard thing we do in our lives, we do in community. I realized that I had tried to solo a lot of my life. As I smudged and placed my prayers held in pinches of tobacco clothed in tiny cotton squares Id cut hundreds of 1 ½ x 1 ½ inch squares of cotton as part of my pre-dance preparations. I was reminded of praying with my mom the morning she was murdered. Although I'd balked at the initial number of prayer ties I was requested to make (the number can vary according to the particular Sundance or tradition or guidance given), I slowly became grateful. Every square and prayer reminded me that, despite my mother's death and my initial belief that prayer was ineffective, the many years (and prayers) since that time had shown me otherwise.

I began to learn what was missing from the course I'd taken at

Naropa: that true, traditional vision quests involve going without food and water for typically four days and nights. In most indigenous cultures, this ceremony is considered a right of passage for boys coming of age; however many cultures now embrace girls and sometimes non-natives who are seeking. The vision quester sits alone, after being 'put up on the hill' as it's often called, praying and crying out to the spirits for a vision to guide them towards their purpose in life and the way in which they are meant to serve the People. Visions may come in the way of dreams and symbolism that must be interpreted by an Elder. Traditionally, the Elders of the Native American cultures designate the sacred vision quest site. Often the same sites have been used for many generations.

Throughout my life I've been thirsty: for a beer at the end of a day of waitressing, thirsty in sobriety for relief of the relentlessness of reality, thirsting for love... But it wasn't until the second day of my first year sundancing that I really experienced thirst. The sun was directly overhead and at least thirty degrees hotter than the nearly iced over morning dew that glistened on every blade of grass outside of the sundance arbor. The sun had sucked up every drop and felt as though it was vacuum sealing my skin and my tongue to the inside of my mouth. I began to have demonic thoughts as I gazed longingly at a tarp sagging beneath the weight of at least a pound of water on the opposite side of the arbor. The tarp was meant to shade the supporters as they danced on the outer circle of the sundance; their movements symbolic of their prayers to give us dancers encouragement and energy. So it didn't matter that the top of the tarp, beneath the pool of water, was slick and black with what must have been oil. In my current state, my eyes began darting to the right, then all the way to the left, without moving my head, to see who was around. I was scheming for ways I could stick my face on that tarp and inhale the water. And the oil, I didn't care. My cells were screaming for hydration and I was ready to do absolutely anything; the sincere petition I'd given to the Sundance Leader when I requested permission to dance was the farthest thing from my mind.

Typically female sundancers will have a female elder to whom they can confess such thoughts and get reprieve by hearing the elder's experience, strength and hope. I knew going into this Sundance that I would be the only woman. And though I relished that at the time, I was now nearly as desperate for female companionship as I was for water.

Just at that moment, I had the distinct sensation that fresh, cool lemonade was blessing the back of my throat, giving the thirst in my mouth a brief reprieve far more than the pebbles we could suck on to keep saliva generating in our mouths. And far more satisfying than the bitter bear root chunks we could occasionally chew on. I had no idea at the time, but later, when the sundance ended, my friends who'd been there to support me shared with me that they had seen how difficult the dance seemed halfway through the second day. They went back to their nearby camp, made fresh lemonade, and drank it as they prayed for me.

Every time I felt as though I was about to pass out, there was a hand extended my way, fanning me with a hawk wing fashioned into a fan through the traditional ways. I learned to turn my attention to others and provide some relief in kind, which inevitably relieved my suffering as well. When a single drum beat signaled preparation for the next round of dancing, I learned how to line up, how to stand up and begin dancing. It was in those moments that I learned to show up and be true to my word.

Only by kissing the gates of death did I begin to understand how to live.

Ironically, being in an altered state of thirst, hunger and exhaustion, I felt the opposite of drunk. In fact, Sundance is the only place in my life where everything felt like it made sense. Even though the ceremony was conducted in a language I didn't fluently speak, I followed every step of the ritual, occasionally without knowledge of why things were done in a particular protocol.

What I couldn't know, until I actually completed my four-year commitment, is what the word "sacrifice" truly means: to make sacred. By sacrificing my need for food and water, along with others making the same sacrifice, I'd cultivate a deeper relationship with the sanctity of water, of food, and especially, of needing and helping other people.

CHAPTER 22

I had to go all the way to India to find forgiveness.

"The journey is called a yatra, a spiritual quest," I could almost see the words hang in the air as my first Sanskrit teacher, Kari, paused. Her rose tinted lips were still curled into an oval shape from the beginning of the word, "quest". I noticed she placed her tongue between her slightly parted teeth to create the "t" sound- just like she'd taught us over a year ago as we began learning how to properly pronounce each of the fifty letters in the Sanskrit Alphabet. Like many clueless plunges I've taken in my life, this class was one of them. In the Fall of 2007, I had been seduced into registering for, "Sanskrit for Yoga Teachers: an 18 month immersion." The most seductive was the word, "immersion"; I imagined myself glistening in a hot spring of Sanskrit.

"Those who travel to the four sacred sites, are thus called 'yatris'," Kari's sing-songy voice continued.

Although I love to travel, India has never been on my bucket list. I knew bits and pieces: it was situated in South Asia and had one of the largest populations, second only to China. But it wasn't until my second day in India that I began to encounter the chaotic, filthy, beautiful and relentlessly real country. It was well over one hundred degrees as our white van chugged up the narrow dirt road. We were slowly dodging cattle and hoards of yatris, many making the sacred trek on foot. "The whole of India comes to take this very, very spiritual journey," our guide Dinesh exclaimed. I wondered how he could be so full of gusto wearing long dark pants, a button down shirt and sweater vest. All of a sudden, the van came to a halt, along with everyone else surrounding us. Out of nowhere appeared young men with shawls for sale, others had beaded jewelry. Families were pulling out camp stoves and preparing tea and food. There was an immediate acceptance to the delay that would be unheard of in the States. It was like an instant diorama and perhaps the only chance I might have to relieve myself. "Dinesh, excuse me, may I go to the bathroom?" "Sure, sure! Go quickly since we may start moving" he said, his accent thick with the British influence that predominated India's recent history.

As I stepped out of the van and onto the dirt, I scanned my options. To the right side of the road was a sheer drop off, and to the left, a steep incline. It looked as though every living thing had utilized that incline as it's bathroom. Since India, and most of South Asia, forgo toilet paper (using their left hands for wiping and reserving the right hand for eating, shaking hands, offering and receiving things from one another), the hillside was covered in poo. I searched desperately for any sight of clean grass or dirt on which to tiptoe up in my flip flops. India is not a country in which they feign politeness and I could feel many eyes on me. That meant I had to keep climbing in hopes of finding an obscure place to go. Sweating through the layers of my lilac colored salwar kameez and shawl draped over my head, I finally made it to a bit of a plateau that seemed hidden from the road's view. After the production of making sure that all of my garments were in their proper place and the zip lock bag I'd brought for my toilet paper and wipes was tucked back in my waistband (I could not get on board with the eastern way of hygiene), I tiptoed my way to head back down the incline. Just as quickly as the sudden city had appeared, and stayed static, our van had begun moving!

Terrified of being left on poo hill, I picked up my pace and began running right over and through the piles of dung. When one of my feet landed on what must have been a recent deposit on the hillside, I slipped. Like the long water slide at Elitch Gardens, I was rapidly sliding downwards, flipping on my side, then my belly as I attempted to stop myself. Only this wasn't a joyride slide at an amusement park. This was a hot, disgusting shit slide. On other people's poop!

Before I'd left for India, I vowed to respect the cultural norms of which Kari had done her best to impart. I knew to leave shoes outside of any temple or holy place we went in, to keep my shoulders and head covered and not to swear. As natural as a knee jerk reflex to a doctor's tiny rubber hammer, I began cursing like a sailor as I flailed down the shit hill. Never before uttered combinations of foul language escaped my lips and didn't stop when my butt finally hit the edge of the road. The van slowed as I ran up to it and the driver opened the pneumatic door, like a school bus. "Sir," I gasped for air, "could I please get my luggage to change?" His face looked as though he was preparing for a shit storm about to come his way, "Mam, I am sorry, but luggage is tied up on top of the van, we cannot get for you right now."

As my fellow Yatris alternated between sympathizing and cutting jokes, I sulked in my seat. Dinesh turned to us after talking with the driver in rapid fire Hindi, "We must turn off the air conditioner, the engine is overheating and will do better to climb this hill without working so hard." If I hadn't been so miserable, I would have appreciated the way in which he acknowledged how hard the engine was working on our behalf. But as soon as we opened the windows, a handful of flies began having a heyday on me. I could feel a steady stream of sweat trickling down my back and pooling beneath my seat. In the world of motorcycling, we call this phenomenon, "swamp ass" in recognition that regardless of how hot the air or the engine, we ride. There's even a powder remedy called "monkey butt" to relieve it.

I looked out the window with a snarl on my face thinking, *There's not enough monkey butt to save this assy situation. This sucks. Why was this ever a good idea to come?* Then my eyes landed on an elderly woman, bent over, her torso almost horizontal, walking barefoot with her hand on a young man's back. She appeared to be smiling. As I looked more closely, I realized she was blind. At that moment, I got it. This woman, with her failing body, was the perfect embodiment of a willingness to go to any lengths to finally achieve closure, forgiveness and the freedom that brings.

Wiping the tears from my eyes, I noticed Dinesh had witnessed what just humbled me. He said gently, "Many must wait their whole lives to be able to take this Yatra. It is believed if your feet touch the earth on the journey, each step brings you closer to the Divine. And if you die along the way, it is a very auspicious blessing."

That's what India does: it removes all the false pretenses, all the resistance to what is sacred, using even shit as fertilizer for those lessons we desperately need. Halfway around the world, I'd discovered the perfect antidote to the City of Beautiful Homes. I had no idea at the time that my immersion in Sanskrit would be a keystone in my unintentional quest for forgiveness.

CHAPTER 23

I wished I could reach out and touch the box with his ashes as it was carried at the head of the procession. The sun was beginning to rise over the eastern horizon, illuminating the sky with a yellow shock of light. It was the third morning of my fourth year of Sundance. When I'd made the commitment to be a sundancer, it never occurred to me that Frank wouldn't see me complete my four year commitment.

A few months earlier, I dipped the hospital sponge into the glass of cool ice water beside Frank's bed and brought it to his lips. I willed my gaze to steady on his freshly trimmed hair and not at the sight of his diaper becoming more visible as the starched top sheet slipped down. I wondered how long he'd have to rest after the exertion of sucking out a few droplets from the sponge. Frank lifted his head, looked right at me and giggled. "I'm wearing diapers! Isn't that funny?" His brown eyes, that always reminded me of a baby seal's, were once again lucid. This small gesture of trying to relieve at least a bit of Frank's thirst made me ponder how he always seemed to meet suffering with such light heartedness.

One large tear escaped, leaving a little stream on the left side of my face. Frank lifted his hand, still strong, though the rest of his body was emaciated, to wipe it away. He didn't have the energy to say any more at that moment, but he didn't need to. Frank's choices said it all. When we spoke on the phone a month ago, he sounded weary and tired, even though he'd been receiving regular dialysis which previously "gave him a little extra pep" as he described it. As the dialysis treatments became needed more frequently, he rented a studio apartment across the street from the Abbotsford Regional Hospital. The commute had become too treacherous with the unpredictable weather in Fraser Valley, British Columbia, for Frank to get rides from the double wide trailer in Agassiz, where he stayed with a kindhearted friend, Martha, her three dogs and slew of cats. Frank, his voice full of gratitude, said, "Those sweet nurses come and pick me up a half hour before each of my dialysis appointments and wheel me over. They love popping wheelies!" I knew he must enjoy flirting with them in his harmless, affectionate way.

Martha called me early on a Wednesday morning in June, 2012. Just finishing my morning meditation practice, I felt as though I was ready to take on the world. Martha's tone sounded tighter than usual. Her voice reminded me of the way she wore her waist-length silver streaked reddish hair tightly bound into a bun, like a librarian. "Lisa, I'm calling to tell you something," although her voice was crisp, I knew how deeply she cared about me. "Frank asked me to call you and let you know he decided to go off dialysis. He said to tell you that he really would have liked to call you himself," I thought I heard her sigh, "but the doctors estimate that, without dialysis he may have only about five days left to live." To calm my emotions, I tried to keep my mind on her Edmonton pronunciation of 'about' with an emphasis on the, 'ow-t', but the phrase 'five days left to live' kept ringing over and over in my head.

With great haste I made arrangements to get work covered, a dog sitter for my eighteen month old Husky, Mato and make travel plans. Having experienced the sudden loss of both of my biological parents, I thought I might be a bit more adept when Frank's time came. This was way different; no amount of meditation and prayer could soften what felt like raw, splintery edges. My friend Cathie refers to the emotional aspects of losing those we love as, "grief soup." All the losses we've ever suffered flood together and with our hearts we 'taste' every single one of them all over again.

I wouldn't know the extent of the people whose lives Frank had touched, until I was sitting in his hospital room just off Highway 1. I'd flown into Seattle, Washington and rented a grey colored Hyundai to drive the two and a half hours on the I-5 N to Abbotsford. Although it was by no means turbo, I knew Frank would appreciate my mode of transportation: Hyundai means "modern times" in Korean. He had a way of maintaining balance between his appreciation for modernization and reverence for 'the old ways'. We both agreed that when it came to music, we much preferred the traditional native songs at Sundance and Pow Wows, as well as songs of the 70's, 80's and Motown on the radio. But when it came to autos, we both loved classic cars, as well as the powerful modern day mustangs and motorcycles. About a year after Frank adopted me, I sent him a Harley Davidson zip up hoodie that he always had tucked in the side of his wheelchair.

My friend Rena met me outside Abbotsford Regional Hospital. Her two kids, twins, now eight years old, called Frank "Mooshum", which means grandpa in Cree. I loved Rena from the moment she and her then three year-old twins bounded up to me at a Sundance in Montana. They were handing out bundles of fresh lilac picked from their field and wrapped in purple ribbon to everyone at Sundance. Rena and I quickly bonded as we discovered we were both much like lilac bushes; we needed a lot of space to grow. Frank facilitated that for each of us and I relished the connection.

Frank had a way of making everyone feel uniquely special and showed that love is never in short supply. Even to the compost pail. A few years back, I drove my van from Colorado to Agassiz, BC to visit Frank at Martha's place. I thought I heard him in the kitchen talking to himself, I walked slowly down the hallway of the trailer, from the front door, past the tiny bathroom and living room, to the linoleum lined kitchen. Frank's back was to me, his spine extending from his wheelchair as his outstretched arms held the plastic compost pail a few inches above his head. "I want you to know how much I appreciate what you do. You sit there quietly on the counter while people toss things your way. You're the silent vessel that holds the fertilizer for our delicious vegetables. Thank you."

When I arrived at the hospital, Rena led me upstairs and motioned towards Frank's room so that I could have a moment alone with him. As I walked through the doorway, he exclaimed, "Oh, my baby, you're *here!* Thank you, thank you for coming," he patted the space next to his frail frame for me to sit beside him and reached for my hand. The Harley hoodie was draped over the back of the chair next to the metal side rails of his hospital bed.

For the next week I was there, nurses popped in and out to see if Frank was awake, to ask if he wanted to speak to so-and-so from Germany / Australia/ Mexico and on and on. When he was resting, I most cherished the coffee runs I'd make with two of the Canadian men Frank had mentored, Andrew and Gray. They taught me how to really drink coffee: quadruple long shots of espresso with a teeny bit of water and half and half. Frank's role to me had been of a father. But now I had the opportunity to see how he served as a teacher and a spiritual guide in the Native Ways to many people: men and women of all ages, races and backgrounds who'd serendipitously found their way to him.

Andrew, Gray, Frank's daughter Lynne and I took shifts sleeping on the twin sized mattress the hospital put in Frank's room for us. Being there, with brief breaks for coffee or to grab food, helped alleviate my fear of losing Frank. It would have devastated me to not show up for him, for this. But I began to get anxious about the cost for all of Frank's hospitalization and treatments. "Andrew, can you help me find out about expenses?" I asked him as we walked the two blocks from Starbucks to the hospital. He turned to look at me as if I was joking. "Oh, you don't know? In Canada we have a publicly funded health care system which means that all of Frank's expenses are covered. Particularly since he worked as a liaison between the penitentiaries and First Nations' rights." "Wow!" I exclaimed, loving Canada and Frank more than ever. He would always boast about the work that others did to benefit his First Nations people, but never about the work he did.

The air in the hospital room was stagnant when Andrew and I walked in from our coffee break. Frank was propped upright in the hospital bed, his eyes looking sad and weary in a way I'd not seen. Andrew waved goodbye as he headed to his hotel room to let out his dog. I was about to go back outside but Frank motioned me to come sit. He was saying to his youngest daughter, "I know you're angry because of things I said and did that hurt you. The time to get that out is now; I don't want you to regret not saying what's on your heart." It was such an intimate conversation. If I was one of Frank's biological daughters I'd probably have some strong feelings about his adopted white girl sitting there, but she nodded her head in my direction, then at the empty chair beside them.

Over the years, I pieced together that at least two of his

daughters (he had four daughters and a son) were intermittently angry with him for the life Frank lived before he got sober and began to live a spiritual life. I always waited for Frank to share things with me and ,out of respect, I never asked questions. His children were all grown, in their 30's to early 40's, and had experienced over half of their lives with him sober and walking a spiritual path. This made me wonder what he'd done and why they were often still angry with him.

His daughter was turned to the side, conveying that she was only half listening to him. Her shiny black hair fell over her shoulders and covered most of her back. From the side, it was obvious she was Frank's daughter. I wondered what features and characteristics she had of her mother's and how old she was when her mother passed away. As she started to sob, I desperately wanted to put my arm around her. But I stayed put, the backs of my thighs stuck to the pleather seat cushion of the hospital easy chair just inches from Frank. The fact that Frank wanted me there shed light on an idea I'd never entertained: perhaps the relationship I had with him wasn't only beneficial to me. I so often basked in the care and attention he gave to me that I'd never received from my own father, it never dawned on me that he may have been receiving something similar. In certain stories he shared with me, I gathered that some of his children struggled with drug and alcohol abuse and, due to active addiction, their actions weren't always trustworthy. Frank knew that it'd been many years since I had any mind altering substances and would often acknowledge the path I was on. One of the things I trusted about him, was that he was a man who'd worked hard to change his ways and be accountable for his actions.

Just a month and a half had passed since Frank was in hospice.

The five days prognosis he'd been given to live post-dialysis had grown into two weeks. I sensed he wanted to make sure there were no stones left unturned; that everyone in his family and his life were as much at peace as possible with his passing. The only word that comes close to describing Frank and the way in which he lived and died is the Sanskrit word, "purna". It's translated to mean fullness, but more broadly conveys the essence of abundance. There's a Sanskrit chant called Purnamadah Purnamidam often used as a blessing before meals that says, "when we subtract fullness from fullness, we're left with fullness." Frank taught me that it doesn't have to be the physical parents and the biological ties that give us what we need.

CHAPTER 24

On a Tuesday morning in May of 2012, The Boulder Public Library left me a voicemail saying that the microfiche I'd ordered had arrived. My editor and I hugged in front of the library entrance.

"You ready?" he asked softly.

"Yeah, I guess, ready as I'll ever be." I said.

I knew I couldn't do this alone and was glad he didn't let me. With both of our armloads full of microfiche (*microfiche!*) we headed to a small windowless room in the northwest corner on the second floor of the library. Freeing a hand, Max opened the tall door to the room marked, "Viewing Room". I took a deep breath.

Seated on hard plastic library chairs, Max turned to me, "Honey, you sure you're ready for this?" he asked again. Most other men calling me "honey" would've creeped me out, but from the moment I'd met Max in 2006, I knew I could trust this guy. Three people from completely different circles in my life had recommended I meet Max when I'd shared with them that I felt like I had a book in me that was itching to come out.

After months of writing, "Email Max" on my daily To Do List, we finally met at the Dushanbe Teahouse on an unusually over-cast June afternoon in Boulder. Amidst the hand-carved wooden pillars that stood like Redwoods holding up a sky of intricately painted tiles, I told Max a nutshell version of my life's story and asked if he'd write the book for me.

Back at that first meeting in 2006, I didn't realize the symbolism of meeting in such a place. The Dushanbe Teahouse was gifted to Boulder by many artisans of Tajikistan who hand-carved and hand-painted the ceramic panels, ceiling tiles, columns, tables and stools. The skills used to create the decorative elements are passed down from generation to generation within families. It is a place where one's lineage is painted beautifully onto every surface. It's a place where you can't avoid history, even your own.

When I asked him to write the book for me, Max's response earned him at least a lifetime of my respect, "I'm sure you could find someone who would do that for you." he said "And who'd do a good job of it. But if you'd like to work with me, I'll teach you everything I know about how to craft a book. It seems like it could be important to have this book come from your own voice."

Sitting together in the library, Max and I followed the trail of old newspaper stories that led to every aspect of my father's arrest and trials. We found on-line case trial research, and we discovered a lot of details. Along with the information I had always guessed (the endless front-page stories that showed our small town's fascination with such a brutal crime), I also discovered information from my father's trial transcripts that had always been hidden from me.

My father's legal team built his defense on the plea that he suffered from a type of temporary insanity, called Intermittent Explosive Disorder, in which he had no forethought or awareness of what he was doing. But the prosecution eventually revealed new evidence. In his last trial, they revealed that prior to my moms murder, my father had stolen powerful narcotic medicines from his pathology lab and hidden them in the trunk of his car. There was also a newspaper clipping found next to his bed, describing another doctor who had drugged and killed his wife and was arrested for the crime. The story that had always been told was that he was momentarily insane when he killed my mother and had no idea what he was doing. But now, five years after my father's death, everything I had known changed. All of the clues pointed towards premeditation.

The feeling in my body was a strange one. My instincts had finally been validated. A part of me always knew there had to be elements of premeditation in my father's actions. I knew him to be calculated, brilliant, manipulative, and driven to have the last word. All of that intelligence paired with an uncontrollable temper, left room for anything to be possible. Sitting in the viewing room, my mind began to buzz with a chill as if I'd just inhaled a pint of ice cream.

And the money. I finally learned the whole truth about how my father spent my mom's money to fund his own defense after killing her. After spending over a month in St. Francis Medical Center, (an abundant amount of time in my opinion) for cuts on his thumb and hand that could likely have occurred from knife slippage from any of the twenty seven stab wounds my mother incurred, my father was freed on a $30,000 Bond. During his hospital stay, a Judge ruled that my parents' divorce, filed on Nov. 11, 1984, just three weeks prior to my mom's death, was never final, due to some technicality. Therefore, my father could legally use my mom's assets to pay his way out of jail for her murder. He was first sentenced to thirty years. He ended up only serving six. Somewhere in that first year of incarceration he was granted freedom to attend my sister Sue's wedding in March of 1985.

The bulk of the documents and transcripts printed out that day filled an entire three-ring binder. For the longest time that binder sat on Max's bookshelf because I couldn't bear to read any of the content. What I eventually did read, haunted me. The details of what really happened on the day my mom was killed came together like an awful photograph that had taken thirty years to develop. In a transcript from the Illinois Supreme Court, I learned things I had never known, things that changed that picture in my mind forever. The knife that killed my mom stayed lodged in her chest as she lay on the floor of the closet. After stabbing my mother twenty seven times, my father fell on top of her and continued to lay on top of her body, until he was forcibly removed by the paramedics and the police.

When I read the line, "a knife was embedded in her left chest," I gasped. Not out loud. I wish it'd been out loud. But an internal gasp that got stuck in my throat. My mind was choking on that image, on the realization that my mom died with a knife in her heart, with my father, her murderer, lying on top of her.

The tears burst out and I didn't try to stop them, a dam had been broken; they gushed over my cheekbones and down my neck. This seemingly simple act of allowing (tears, facts, images) is at the heart of forgiveness. My two parents are the only ones who know what really happened that day and why, and they are both gone. Allowing the truth of that reality to settle in has enabled me to see that true forgiveness must encompass all possible pasts, in order to allow for a real future. Forgiveness isn't just a nice idea. It isn't about forgetting or condoning. It is my only path out of a lifetime of suffering.

I've heard it said that healing begins with forgiveness. But that wasn't my experience. For me, healing began with learning how to feel rage in ways that didn't harm others or myself. For many years I found anger empowering; in the end I realized that anger was simply too large a burden to carry. As the poet Marge Piercy once wrote, "because anger is a fire that must be fed and we are too tired to rise and haul a log."

Beneath my anger was a deep reservoir of sadness: sadness for my mom not getting to live a full life, for myself as a mother-less daughter, sadness for all the motherless daughters, sadness for my dad never being the father I so desperately wanted him to be, sadness for this dreadful legacy in our family. And that list just barely scratched the surface.

I used to believe that anger was a form of strength. I tried to cultivate outer strength through bodybuilding and driving powerful cars and motorcycles, and by perfecting my emotional icy stare. I tried to cultivate inner strength through sundancing and waking up at 4am to study Sanskrit for hours on end. I also cultivated it by doing the introspective work of looking at my defects and the beliefs that no longer served me.

One of the beliefs I clung to was that I needed my father to apologize in order for me to forgive him. Like trying to get blood from a stone, no amount of pleading or prodding could extract what I thought I needed in order to be free. He never actually said he was sorry. And I was incarcerated by this belief. But some-thing my Sanskrit teacher, Manorama said to me rang in my ear, "How do you take the experiences of your life and make them your prayer wheel?"

Over the course of my life, the notion of prayer has filled the spectrum from disdain to skepticism and on to full fledged faith. Rather than a linear progression, my belief in the power of prayer has a fluidity that persists along that spectrum. My first memories of praying began around age seven and continued through age eleven, when my only daily prayer was for my dad to stop beating my mom. I once prayed for a Cabbage Patch Kid. We prayed at the Passover table, but this was a series of fast reading so we could eat. I thought of prayer as a way to focus on something honorable (mom, dolls, food), so God, (*maybe Morgan Freeman?*), or whomever fielded all the prayer requests, would more likely consider granting it.

Just three days after my twelfth birthday, when the opposite of my prayers happened and my father's violence consumed my mom's life, I immediately flipped God the bird. I didn't necessarily stop believing that there was a higher power or divine force; I just stopped believing that "it" gave a shit about me and my prayers.

During my headfirst plunge into the darkness of the next decade of my life, spent mostly drunk or figuring out ways to get drunk, my only prayers were of the foxhole-in-the-middle-of-battle variety: "God, I swear, if you get me out of this, I'll stop lying and stealing." But as quickly as those desperate prayers were spoken, I'd dismiss them, lying and stealing all over again. Just after I'd turned twenty, in the thick chill of Chicago's December, I stole my roommate's hand knit Irish sweater and then guilelessly helped her "look for it" when she discovered it missing.

But thirty two months later, after I'd celebrated an entire year, including weekends, without alcohol or mind-altering substances, I wrote that roommate a letter (and returned the sweater) owning up to my thievery and deception and asked how I could right this wrong. Her letter in response was simply to congratulate me for having the courage to clean up that situation. As I read her generosity, I loudly proclaimed to the late August heat of my Colorado apartment, "Thank you God!" So clearly I believed in something.

These days I think of praying like vacuuming. I need to clear away all the dust and dog hair that clouds my thinking that I am any degree superior or inferior to anyone else; clear the space so that I can see, with the clean carpet of my mind, how we all have the best and worst inside of ourselves. I can't mention carpets without thinking of Stuart Smalley, "it's easier to put on slippers than to carpet the entire world." It's both that simple and profound: when I place my attention on what I can become aware of and change about myself, I suffer less. Forgiveness is the practice of freeing myself from the prison I create out of my own resentment.

I really didn't know what the hell Manorama meant when she suggested I take the experiences of my life and make them into my prayer wheel. But I continued to lean into this question. I knew that prayer wheels are beautiful and physical, that they are native to Tibetan Buddhism. They have been around a long ass time, since around the 4th century and in fact the concept of a prayer wheel comes from Buddha's teaching method, "turning the wheel of dharma." Dharma refers to law and order (not the TV show), and refers both to one's purpose in life as well as to how that personal direction serves the greater, universal whole. Like the way that every drop of water contributes to the magnificence of the ocean.

The truth was that, while I had never considered turning my life into a prayer wheel, I knew all about wheels and the power of motion. In grade school I wrote a poem about "wind warriors who found freedom two-wheelin on freeways", pretty heady stuff for a kid just learning to ride a bicycle. Shortly after I got my driver's license at the age of twenty five (I wanted to wait a few years to see if the staying sober thing stuck), I took a weekend "Learn to Ride a Motorcycle" course at a community college in Westminster, Colorado. Out of seventeen people in the class, I was one of the few who didn't drop the 250 cc bikes we maneuvered around orange construction cones in the football field sized parking lot. I quickly became fond of the only bright yellow Easy Rider style helmet, and the course instructor quickly became fond of calling me "Sunshine". Shockingly, I passed the class. Awarded a motorcycle endorsement on my driver's license and a discount on my insurance, I promptly purchased my first Harley Davidson.

I was devastated to discover that I was terrified of driving a vehicle with two wheels and a v-twin engine. Even in the empty parking lot of the local Kentucky Fried Chicken, I realized that I would need something to soothe my rattled ego and my nerves if I was going to stay on the bike and stay alive. I was simultaneously learning to ride a motorcycle and learning Sanskrit. While practicing starting, stopping, shifting and turning, all with a huge rumbling engine underneath me, I began to chant mantras of protection and safety. I chanted the Sanskrit alphabet and any invocations I could think of. It was more like shouting than chanting, usually inside my helmet. While it's not recommended that one practice those sacred sounds in moving vehicles, the repetition helped me to focus on something other than my own fear. Those motorcycle mantras eventually took me and my bike all over the U.S., through ten National Parks (in one trip!) and up to Sundance in Manitoba, Canada.

Prayer is one of the many ways I've learned to hold myself on the earth. It forces me into self-examination and introspection and has been one of the invisible bridges to forgiveness. My teacher Manorama was keen on giving me specific homework tasks that seemed to have zero association to my learning and practicing Sanskrit. One time she told me to write all the qualities that I admired and hated about both of my parents and then write which of those qualities I recognize in myself. "I don't mean to be irreverent," I said apprehensively, "but I'm wondering what the connection is between the homework assignment and my learning

Sanskrit?" With Yoda-like wisdom, she responded, "Everything we are, is in everything we do." And, annoyingly, she was right.

I had to learn about myself in order to begin to understand and have compassion for others, and compassion for my father. Like when someone cuts me off in traffic, I can only be pissed at them until the point at which I recall the numerous times that I've been the a-hole cutting someone else off to get a car or two ahead. When I follow those types of threads, forgiveness becomes available.

CHAPTER 25

I frickin' hate Tinder.

But I loved the line in Chris's profile that read, "My mom hopes I meet someone nice on here." Reading it, I thought, *either this guy is a total player like most of the cybermen I've connected with; or he's a total momma's boy, or maybe there's a 1% chance that he's for real.*

Notoriously an online hook-up site (where mates or dates are chosen or rejected by a swipe of the finger on a screen) Tinder is scary but occasionally useful. After more than a decade of online dating (broken by brief interludes of swearing I'd never ever ever Ever do that again), as the summer of 2015 was winding down, I decided to give it one more try.

Because of my parents incredibly flawed examples of what love and relationships should look like, I decided to create my own rules for finding love that, at the very least, were hilarious enough to make me feel better about not having met the 'right' guy (yet):

1. No dating students in any of my yoga classes: a solid vow "not to get my honey where I get my money"

2. No dating students in any of the yoga studios in which I taught and practiced

3. No dating anyone from any of my spiritual communities

4. No dating neighbors

5. No dating anyone who lived in a five mile radius of my house.

6. No dating anyone just because I liked their British accent.

7. No dating anyone who had my dream motorcycle

8. No dating anyone who looks like Clark Kent

9. No dating anyone who needs drugs or alcohol to have a good time

With all these rules, there were probably two guys (throughout the continental U.S.) and one guy in a cave in Antarctica who made the cut. And since the cave dweller probably had no internet access and I had exhausted Match.com, I took to Tinder.

As I scrolled through the photos on Chris's profile, I was struck by one in particular. It showed him holding the hand of a young girl, maybe three years old. Her tiny hand stuck out of an equally small yellow baby chicken costume and although they were walking away from the camera, I could see the profile of her big smile as she looked at him. The skeptic in me immediately thought that maybe he rented a cute kid for the photo, but there was something that tugged at my curiosity. We messaged back and forth a few times, during which I learned that the kid was indeed his. I dropped my digits in hopes he'd call. It was always important to me to hear someone's voice before we met. I had a somewhat smaller, but equally vital list of requirements for someone's voice that boiled down to this: it can't annoy me. It took him over a week to ring me, but the tone of his voice sounded both sexy and like a comfortable sofa I could rest on.

Over the next two weeks we talked a few more times; I always equated those pre-meeting conversations to the little taster cups from frozen yogurt places: just enough to determine if you want to invest in a bigger serving. I found out that he ran his own Construction/ Home Renovation business, that he was a musician and that he was surprisingly well versed in politics, physics and also played the best sport out there: hockey.

We decided to meet at a restaurant on a Monday evening in late August, breaking my own rule that first meetings need to just be coffee or tea dates, without the pressure of an entire meal. (Just in case we discovered that we couldn't stand each other in the same moment that the appetizers arrived.) As I pulled into a parking spot, I saw him leaning against the wrought iron fence in front of the restaurant we'd chosen in downtown Louisville, Colorado. Dressed in dark denim, his long legs were leisurely crossed at the ankle, a slight smile on his face. I can't remember what I wore, only that I had decided to shower and wash my hair. Another single girlfriend and I joked that the dead give-away of whether we were really interested in meeting someone was if we showered and washed our hair; most of the time, with most of the dates I'd been on, it wasn't worth the effort.

Chris and I hugged hello and I noticed that his thick dark hair smelled wonderful.

"It's nice to meet you," he said. His voice already felt so familiar.

"You too!" I noticed how the olive green of his shirt complimented flecks in his brown eyes.

"So, the restaurant we planned to go to is closed..." he paused.

(I decided not to interpret this as a sign.) "But there's an Italian restaurant a few doors down, would that be okay?"

Thank God the service at the Italian place sucked because

it gave us something to joke about, and an excuse to have a 3 hour long dinner. Our conversation ranged from music preferences to his divorce (over three years ago) to how bridges are constructed.

What was different about dating Chris was that it wasn't the same fever of talking every night until 3 a.m.; it wasn't a crazy-kid-frantic thing. It was immediately grown up without the slightest hint of boring. I began to see and trust that the greatest priority in his life is his daughter. And unlike a few friends of mine who felt threatened by being second in a man's heart, I began to love that his role as a father created many of the qualities I cherished. But no sooner had I begun to trust that Chris was exactly who he said he was, than I found myself relapsing into the old fear that men can't be trusted.

In a moment gripped by an overwhelming fear and insecurity, I figured out the password to his phone, noticing the pattern out of the corner of my eye as he typed it in. Then, when he was in the bathroom, I accessed and scrolled through his text messages. And of course I found nothing. Unable to live with the shame and guilt of betraying his trust, I confessed to Chris. Moments like that showed me how level-headed he was, able to calmly and honestly address conflict between us and work through it. Ironically, it was through my own insecurities and foibles that I began to trust him.

The one thing I was totally unprepared for was the deep and honest connection Chris has with his family. We'd been dating about half a year when he invited me to come to Florida where his parents, his brothers and their families were gathering after the holidays. A couple of weeks before our scheduled departure, I received an email that said:

Dear Lisa,

I am Chris's mom and just wanted to introduce myself and welcome you to our family reunion at Christmas time. Hopefully I am not out of line for doing this, but my maternal curiosity forced me to look up "Lisa, paddle board yoga" to see who this person is that Chris has invited to join us. You are an excellent writer and I've enjoyed reading through your website, especially your blog. We look forward to meeting you and since my two daughters-in-law and I dabble in yoga, perhaps we can sneak away on the beach and enjoy your expertise.

Looking forward to meeting you.
Pat

Holy shit! I thought, *Chris's mom read all about me; what does she think about this book, about my less than normal life, and her son dating someone with my family history? Why do I always forget about the fact that anyone can Google me?*

By the time I got to Florida, I realized that I had nothing to worry about. Pat and the rest of Chris's family welcomed me and made me feel normal and cared for. I didn't expect to feel so comfortable with them, but I did. Still, nothing could have prepared myself for falling in love with his then eight year-old daughter, Hayley. After Chris and I decided to date exclusively, the three of us went to an Avalanche hockey game. It was the first time I met her and she was understandably shy and a bit apprehensive. But we quickly became buddies, practicing cart-wheels and handstands in the grass in front of their condo and giggling as we read stories before bedtime. The gift of connecting with a child gave me a do-over on my own amputated childhood, and the wildly unexpected chance to be a mother figure to an amazing kid. I often said to Chris and Hayley that I got a 'two-fer'; I got the bonus of two incredible humans for the price of one.

I know that there are profound losses in our lives, like the loss of my mom, that we never entirely heal from. But as I spent more and more time with Chris and Hayley, I began to realize that I had healed enough that I was ready to step into loving them with my whole heart and to take on the semi- parenting role that Hayley was inviting me into. When Frank was on his death-bed, I had discovered that our long chosen-parent/chosen-child rela-tionship had been a life changing gift to us both. In loving Hayley, I discovered the same thing; I thought I was just receiving a gift but I realized that I was giving one as well. Our relationship as a new family was like all relationships; it wasn't always easy but we were trying to figure it out together.

In the early summer of 2017 we hauled the last box into a two story house just steps away from a lake in Lafayette. I had a wonderful space in which to write, Hayley had her own bedroom which she shared with about seventy five stuffed animals. Standing in our new bedroom, I noticed the large window that overlooked the foothills of Boulder. I realized that there was no circumstance in which I would ever have to crawl out of that window to safety. I had finally broken the fears and patterns of the life my mother had lived. On Father's Day that year, Hayley asked me to help her make a Father's Day card. We sat down at her desk and she began to write a poem for Chris. I suggested she name some of the qualities she loves the most about her "dada", as she calls him. The next morning we were all three sitting in our new kitchen together. Chris and I had disagreed about something, (who even knows what) but in the middle of it all Hayley asked me, "what's your favorite thing about my dada?" And in that moment, our disagreement seemed to disappear. I instantly said, "his kindness." And realized that it was true. I had chosen a profoundly kind man and one who loved his child and his family more than any other part of his life. More than being right. More than getting what he wanted. More than having the last word.

One night, after we put Hayley to bed, I had a sudden memory of a letter that my Great-Uncle Leon wrote when he was working as a Physician in Brooklyn. He wrote, "the heart is the only organ in the body that works better after it's broken."

I thought the story would end there; in our loving home starting a new family in the happy-but-messy-ever-after that I never expected to have.

But endings are tricky.

And love, as it turns out, is even trickier. Things can end without shattering or exploding.

Maybe that's what I needed to learn.

After five years in relationship, living and parenting together, Chris and I found that we were compatible in some ways, but not in others. Some of the ways in which we didn't mesh were ones that mattered.

Kindness is a rare and amazing foundation to have with another person, but even a foundation of kindness needs sustained compatibility in order to build a future.

The most incredible thing is that my love for Hayley hasn't dimmed or changed. It turns out that loving a child is a forever proposition, even if you are no longer the person pouring their cereal in the morning. And my love for Chris's mother Pat hasn't dimmed or changed either. With Chris's approval, she and I have continued our relationship. So I am blessed to receive the gift of being loved and mothered by an amazing woman.

Today I think back to the Ganges River and the cola-colored water swirling around my ankles, as it readied to receive my father's ashes. Standing there in that beautiful, filthy, incredible place, I didn't know that I'd have to open my hands and let him go. Not just once, but that I would have to do it again and again and again. Every time someone hurt me, every time I disappointed myself, I would have to open my hands and let go. I know that once my palms are open I can't help but receive. I didn't know that day that letting go could quench my thirst, but now I do.

Forgiveness (what I call, "the new f-word"), much like yoga, is a practice. A lifelong, life changing practice. And helping others learn what forgiveness means and how to do it is my life's calling. Of course I'd be stoked if some aspect of my story ignites a forgiveness revolution; I think we all need an opportunity to look at the places in our lives where resentment or regret holds us back from living our most awesome life.

Somewhere over this long journey I've learned that in our thirst for justice, for nourishment, for love; we will fall again and again and sometimes, we will break.

But every time we break we will learn. My prayer is that we will forgive and find love for others and ourselves.

Then, like delightful idiots, we will do it all over again.

ACKNOWLEDGMENTS

I feel as though this book beckoned me, it began as a tap on the shoulder I could easily brush off, but it evolved into a demanding insistence, one I still tried to shirk. As writer Alice Hoffman wrote, "I've always believed there's a very thin line that separates readers and writers; you make a leap over that line when there's a book you wanna read and you can't find it and you have to write it yourself."

In finally surrendering to this process I've created (with the help of an amazing team) the book I thirsted for when I was twelve. This book is about my journey through perception shifts. It's about learning how to discern the true from the false and my undying desire for healing and evolution.

A thousand loving hands have held me up, especially during my most unlovable years. Thank you to everyone who loved me until I could begin to love myself. You've held a vision for my life in which I've gotta wear my big girl panties and show up! Jeanne (and Bruni!), Melody, Kathy, thank you for being my trinity! Cathie (Fwend), Carolyn, and Annette, your love is my fuel.

Thanks to my book Team: Max Regan, my developmental editor, from the moment of conception of this book, you've been there by my side, sharing all that you know (which is a helluva lot.) Thank you to my sweet and savvy writer's group of memoirists for your brilliant insight, my beta readers for helping to shape this final draft with your feedback, Mark Gelotte, my book designer, Ron Bueker for web wizardry, Pat Vagias, my loving copy editor, and Ali Kennedy, my marketing manager, for going above and waaaay beyond the call of duty.

A shout out to Eddie Vedder/ Pearl Jam, Phil Collins, Beastie Boys, Lauren Daigle, and Alicia Keys for your music, played incessantly, while I was writing and editing.

This project would not have been born without the backing of so, so many; A HUGE Thank You to:

Amanda Leon, Robin Fierer-Wilson, Bill Lomelino, Emily Nozick, Lauren Chassin, Zen Daddy, Susan Connor, Bari Nan Cohen Rothchild, Debra Silverman, Gouri Orekondy, Aunt Cathy Carlson, Sylvie Sherman-Bloch, Stephanie Birkey Reffey, Doug Schnitzpahn, Laura Payne, Janice Little, Nicole & Gerry Weinholt, Amy Whitman, Kat Webb, Rebecca Lafferty, Jenna Vagias, Pat & Jibber Vagias, Eileen Druggish, Don Shephard, Jennifer Emich, Amy Rubin, Jennifer Anderson, Anne Spacone, Trish Morris, Connie Leon, Sarah Looper, Mary Brennan, Derise Anjanette & Matt Kapinus, Peter Hathaway, Deborah Pike, Lisa Akins, Kelly Burton, Natascha Bruckner, John Espinosa, Greyson Kirby, Dr. Cindy Riegel, Liz Amann Whitney, Brooke Turner, Darla McKenzie, Brooke-Lynn Killingbeck, Lindsay Schumacher, Banyan Fierer, Jennifer Kronenberg, Susan Schultz, Ron Bueker, Jessica Lorentz, Bonnie Cole, Scott Munkvold, Stacy Boston, Alison Rogers, Karen Erickson, Jaime Ray, Jennifer Maddox, Pam Simich, Sindee Ernst, Kathleen McLaughlin, Denise Knutson, Dawn Brady, Holly Virden, Kristina Nelleson, Jennifer Davison, Erik Foster, Julie Zanon, Jeffrey McCord, Ben Camacho, and Annette Gagne!

And lastly, thanks to all the men I took hostage, er, dated, while trying to work through my dad-shit. Hopefully this book makes up for a fraction of my assholery.

RESOURCES

Domestic Violence, which is sometimes referred to as DV, is also referred to as Intimate Partner Violence (IPV), dating abuse, or relationship abuse. It is a pattern of behaviors used by one partner to maintain power and control over another partner in an intimate relationship.

Domestic violence doesn't discriminate. People of any race, age, gender, sexuality, religion, education level, or economic status can be a victim — or perpetrator — of domestic violence. That includes behaviors that physically harm, intimidate, manipulate or control a partner, or otherwise force them to behave in ways they don't want to, including through physical violence, threats, emotional abuse, or financial control.

If you or someone you know is afraid, being controlled or harmed or in danger of being harmed, please reach out, there are many resources available to help you, both locally and nationally. **The National Domestic Violence Hotline can be reached at (800)799-SAFE (7233) or online at thehotline.org**

Lisa Fierer is a dynamic speaker, an accredited expert yoga teacher and a Forgiveness Educator. In 15 years of speaking and teaching everywhere from Lululemon to Harley Davidson to Glide, she has inspired over 20,000 people to embrace the power of forgiveness.

With over 1000 hours of yoga training, Lisa strives to guide her students towards the divine wisdom that lies within each and every one of us. Through the doorway of yoga, Lisa began to study Sanskrit. In 2009 Lisa completed an immersion training utilizing Sanskrit in teaching Yoga and now leads Sanskrit Teacher Trainings and Workshops. Lisa has also trained with Matthew Sanford in Adaptive Yoga, which makes yoga accessible to people who are differently-abled. She has taught yoga at Detox Centers, through Phoenix Multisport, bringing the practice to people recovering from substance abuse, and supporting the recovery of body, mind, and spirit. In 2011, Lisa discovered StandUp Paddleboard (SUP) Yoga and earned certifications to teach SUP Yoga & Fitness. As a Master Trainer, she now leads StandUp Paddleboard, SUP Yoga,

& Fitness Teacher Trainings throughout Colorado, the United States, and Internationally.

Through her consulting business Lisa also trains people and companies to cultivate the #1 skill needed to reduce stress and increase productivity: Forgiveness. With her proven method of **Fear Less - Forgive More,** Lisa uses humor, storytelling, and yogic principles to teach people and companies how to let go of debilitating beliefs that hold us back and discover the freedom and joy of life without these bonds.

www.lisafierer.com

Made in the USA
Coppell, TX
07 December 2020

43778935R00142